CW00458556

A GRATITUDE MINDSET FOR TEENS

PRACTICAL LESSONS AND ACTIVITIES TO APPLY MINDFULNESS, MANIFEST SUCCESS, AND CULTIVATE THANKFULNESS IN 31 DAYS

SYDNEY SHEPPARD

CONTENTS

INTRODUCTION

Did you know that expressing gratitude can improve your overall well-being and make you happier? More than 90% of American teens and adults agree with this statement (*10 Amazing Statistics to Celebrate National Gratitude Month*, 2020).

Gratitude is more than just saying "thank you." True gratitude starts from within. It's a feeling of happiness and is directly linked to overall well-being. By practicing gratitude regularly, we can improve every aspect of our lives, which we will discuss in the chapters to come.

Before you decide that this is some "pie-in-the-sky" idea that I'm pitching to you, I know it's difficult. We all have stress that we need to deal with daily, and it's not always possible to feel grateful every second of the day. Not to mention the daily pressures we have to meet expectations, thrive in our personal lives, build and maintain relationships, drink enough water, get a sufficient amount of sleep, exercise, and still do something for our own mental well-being. Trust me—I know that it can be quite overwhelming.

With all these expectations, it's no wonder that most of us have forgotten to *stop and smell the flowers*. It feels like there is no time!

But, what if I told you that you can improve all these things and learn to deal with the pressure in a healthy way? It can be hard to find the balance sometimes, but when we adjust our mindset and really give it the best we got, things will turn around for the better.

Sounds good, right? And I'm sure you already know what mindset I am referring to since it's part of the book title.

A gratitude mindset will change your life more than you can imagine, guaranteed. I am so confident you will benefit from it that I won't even put a disclaimer to say that up to 95% of people reported a change in their life when they adopted a gratitude mindset. That's a completely made-up statistic and absolutely irrelevant because it will make a difference.

Over and above the fact that gratitude makes us feel good in the moment, we can also reap many other benefits by habitually practicing it. We make better decisions, experience more positive emotions, build better relationships, and take positive actions in response to daily challenges.

If you engage meaningfully with this book and apply the tools to your own life, you will benefit from it in the short and long term. Some of the benefits include:

- Gaining a better understanding of gratitude.
- Strategies to shift your current perspective.
- Tools to improve your emotional well-being.
- Effective ways to build and nurture relationships.
- How to bounce back quicker after a setback.
- Tips and tricks for applying gratitude to your daily life.

It should come as no surprise that your overall well-being will improve when you understand and apply the above concepts. You will see an improvement in your mental and physical health, be able to relate to others better to build closer relationships, have enhanced resilience to get you through difficult times, and have improved overall happiness.

I work with teens and young adults daily to help adapt their mindset where needed. The work that I've done over the last few years has really inspired me to start a Mindset Series where I can share some of the techniques and pearls of wisdom with a broader audience. I have two other books that have already been published. The first deals with cultivating a growth mindset and becoming resilient, and the second book discusses developing the right money mindset. Gratitude is the next step.

I know words are just words without any proof. About a year ago, I started working with a teen who was really struggling to manage their day-to-day life. They were having a hard time juggling the exams, uncertainty about their future, and managing their relationships (especially with their parents), and they have been struggling with anxiety, which has manifested in physical symptoms, including heart palpitations. When they came to me at first, the expectation was never to help them with their physical ailments, but as the weeks turned into months, even their physical and mental health improved.

Now, they keep a gratitude journal, and we still check in every now and then. He's a completely new person, and I'm so proud of the journey he's been on. And I want to help you, too!

Everything I taught them I included in this book. Each chapter contains a few activities. You don't need to complete these activities in one day. In fact, you will gain the most out of them if you can practice them more than once and make some part of your daily routine.

Take some time to really understand a concept before you move on to the next. At the end of the book, I have included 31 days of being grateful for you to practice gratitude differently every day.

We start with an overview of gratitude, what it is, why it's so significant, the science behind it, and the relationship between gratitude, happiness, and success. Then we move on to changing our perspective and reframing those negative thoughts to get a better outcome because how are we supposed to be positive if our thoughts are still those of Negative Nancy? A Negative Nancy only sees the bad—everything they say and think is negative, which is definitely not what we're aiming for.

Chapter 3 deals with emotional well-being and how we can overcome depression and anxiety by practicing gratitude. We also talk about stress management and knowing our worth. In the two chapters after that, we look at gratitude's role in nurturing relationships and how we can improve our resilience overall.

In the last part of the book, we look at the impact of gratitude on our physical health and how we can practice and express gratitude daily. Finally, Chapter 9 includes the 31 days of gratitude I mentioned earlier.

This is not just another book that you read from cover to cover without being able to apply any of it. It's a guide to transform your life through the power of gratitude. I understand the struggles that you go through because I work with teens who go through it daily, and I've also been there myself. It's not easy. But we can make a difference together. I'm really excited to walk this journey with you.

Are you ready to change your life?

THE POWER OF GRATITUDE

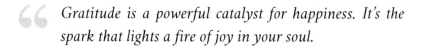 *Gratitude is a powerful catalyst for happiness. It's the spark that lights a fire of joy in your soul.*

— AMY COLLETTE

We all get to a point in life where things feel like they're getting too much, and how we choose to get out of that mindset may differ from person to person. I know of some people who choose to go shopping so that they can feel better, while others allow it to build up and have anger outbursts and everything in between.

There's not really a right or a wrong way to deal with it, but there definitely is a better way to refocus on your goals and recover from whatever life has thrown at you. The two methods I mentioned are damaging to our emotional health, even though shopping might seem harmless.

They also say that venting is healthy because you get rid of all the negative emotions, but what if there was a better way to actually change your perspective and, as a result, improve your overall well-being?

Cultivating a gratitude mindset can do exactly that. If we can focus on being grateful for what we have and appreciating the small things, most things will seem trivial in comparison.

In this chapter, we will take a closer look at what gratitude is and why it's important. There's definitely some scientific evidence to back up what I'm saying, which is covered in the second part of the chapter. And finally, we'll explore any connection between gratitude, happiness, and success. There are also a few gratitude activities to complete after each section.

UNDERSTANDING THE MEANING AND ESSENCE OF GRATITUDE

We've spoken a bit about gratitude now, and I think most people have a good understanding of what gratitude is. Or maybe they think they do. For everyone's benefit, I think we should briefly define what gratitude is.

Simply put, gratitude can probably be most likened to appreciation and being appreciative of certain things in life. Millacci (2023) did quite a bit of research on this because it's more than just appreciating something.

According to her research, although they may fall under the same umbrella, gratitude can be split into two distinct phases and involves more than just one emotion.

The first stage of gratitude consists of the realization that there is good in our lives. Although things may go wrong sometimes, there is always something good around us. We just need to see it. The second stage of gratitude is knowing where this goodness comes from and acknowledging that it's not by our doing. The good things are there because of other people, animals, nature, or a higher power.

Understanding these two steps helps us to realize what we should be thankful for and who we need to thank for those things.

But we still haven't properly defined gratitude. To do that, let's look at some facts linked to gratitude:

- It involves thankfulness and happiness.
- The thankfulness and happiness are felt in response to something that has been received or may have happened.
- There is normally some kind of action that is projected toward someone or something other than ourselves.

Using this, here is a simple definition of gratitude that you can refer back to throughout the book:

Gratitude is feeling happy and thankful toward someone or something in response to an event or gift we received. We can either show gratitude or receive gratitude from others.

Keeping this definition in mind: Remember when you were truly grateful for something? We get so caught up in life and have so many expectations that we feel we deserve these things.

Instead of expressing gratitude, we might feel, "I worked hard for this. I deserve it." We completely miss the blessings in our everyday lives because we feel entitled. And when these blessings, which we feel we are entitled to, do not appear, we might feel angry and discouraged.

For example, if you do well in school, your parents might promise you a new cellphone for your birthday. You've already accepted that you deserve it (if you do well), so when you receive the new cellphone, how do you react? Is it the same as you would have if they just surprised you with it?

In both instances, they give you something new that is really amazing, but simply because you feel like you deserve it, you may not feel the same level of gratitude. Unfortunately, it has become the norm in our society, and this is why we struggle to find things that we can be grateful for.

Here's another scenario. Every morning, I wake up and go on with my day without really thinking about breathing. On the other hand, when someone with lung cancer wakes up, each breath they take feels like a blessing. I take mornings and breathing for granted, but someone who is sick savors every breath as if it's their last. They celebrate every new day. Shouldn't we do that too? Why wait until we're forced to see it as a blessing?

So, what does gratitude do? It helps us to focus on the good things in life. It puts a new and positive spin on our outlook and makes us feel better. It helps us to look forward to every new day and new opportunities we face instead of postponing it until later.

Another thing gratitude does is help us to make friends. I don't know about you, but being around a Negative Nancy who complains about everything is difficult. It's really draining, and I always look for reasons not to hang out with those kinds of people. I would much rather spend my time with positive people—people who see a way forward when things go wrong, will pick me up when I feel like having a pity party, come up with solutions to problems, and have fun no matter what they decide to do. These people know where it's at.

Let's start with some easy activities you can implement in your life today to practice gratitude.

Activity One: Gratitude Journal

This is one of the first steps to help us identify things to be grateful for. All we need to do is write down three things we are grateful for every day. This can be done first thing in the morning to set the tone for the day or even just before bed when reflecting on the day that has passed.

It doesn't have to be a fancy journal, as long as we can write it down somewhere and be able to refer back to it. In saying that, there are also some really amazing options in the market at the moment with the most beautiful designs. I find it much easier to jot down some thoughts in a book that I absolutely adore. It makes me feel happy. If you are the same, make sure that you find a gratitude journal that makes you look forward to reflecting.

By identifying three things each day, we become more aware of the daily blessings we encounter without even thinking twice about them. Being more aware every day can change your life.

Activity Two: Gratitude Walk

This is one of my favorite activities, especially when surrounded by nature. A gratitude walk is exactly that: A walk where you become aware of your surroundings and feel grateful for what nature has to offer.

If you have a nice park nearby or a nice neighborhood, take a mindful walk where you can experience everything the walk offers. Even if it's a path you take every day, I bet you will find things you never noticed!

We tend to get so caught up that we miss the beauty that nature has to offer us. By taking a gratitude walk, we reconnect with nature and our surroundings, which will turn a boring, mundane walk into the most exciting activity of the day.

SCIENTIFIC EVIDENCE SUPPORTING THE POSITIVE IMPACT OF GRATITUDE

I know that the first part may have been sufficient to convince some that gratitude can improve your life; however, others might need to see some statistics and science that back up that claim.

Practicing gratitude has three main benefits: psychological, social, and physical. The psychological and social benefits may be noticed shortly after you start your journey. It might take a little longer for the physical benefits to become evident.

▷ Psychological

Psychologically, it can make you happier. Your mood is automatically lifted, and you become more aware and experience more positive emotions.

Whenever we express gratitude, our brains release our *feel-good* hormones: dopamine and serotonin. This is where that immediate happiness comes from and why it improves our mood almost immediately. The more we express gratitude, the stronger these neural connections get to release these hormones, and the longer the effects will last.

Wong et al. (2018) conducted a study where a group of individuals who required mental health counseling were divided into two categories. Both categories of individuals had regular counseling sessions; however, those in category one were also asked to write gratitude letters throughout the study. The results were shocking! Category one individuals recovered much sooner and felt happier, while the ones in category two still experienced depression and anxiety once the study came to an end.

▷ Social

Looking at the social impact, you become more empathic, a better communicator, and are able to build better relationships with others.

Scientists also believe that gratitude is a socially driven emotion since it directly correlates with how we see ourselves and those around us (Chowdhury, 2019). Those who practice gratitude more often have a more positive perception of what they can offer to and receive from others. This is what helps us build stronger relationships with those around us.

▷ Physical

From a physical aspect, it can improve your physical health, strengthen your immune system, and even improve your sleep.

A number of scientific findings support improved physical health. One that we have already explored is the increased release of dopamine, which can reduce any physical pain that we're feeling and help us to feel more motivated to be active.

By consistently expressing gratitude, we also activate the hypothalamus in our brains. The hypothalamus is responsible for a lot of functions, including emotions, hormone regulation, and sleep. A hypothalamus that functions properly can help us to get a proper night's rest more often than not.

Isn't it amazing?

In addition to this, there seems to also be a structural change in the brains of those who regularly express gratitude. They tend to have more gray matter in their right inferior temporal gyrus (Chowdhury, 2019). This is the part of the brain that mostly deals with memory, sensory integration, language, and visual perception. When you have more gray matter, your brain can send better signals which results in improved functioning.

So, more gray matter in that area improves the functions it's responsible for. Essentially, being grateful makes you smarter and more creative.

Here are some activities that can help us understand the connection of gratitude with the different aspects of our lives.

Activity Three: Gratitude Reflection

This is a quick activity that can be incorporated with Activity One, keeping a gratitude journal. It involves reflecting on your feelings before you jot down your gratitude points and again after you have written them down.

Before you start with your gratitude journal, take a minute or two to reflect on how you are feeling at that moment. Be as specific as possible. Are you excited to write down your points for the day? Are you feeling overwhelmed because you are not sure what to write down? Or maybe you are feeling annoyed that I'm making you do it. Whatever your feelings, name them and write them down if you need to.

Once you have written down your three gratitude points, take a moment to reflect on your feelings again. You might feel completely different. Your feelings might even have made a 180-degree turn. If you wrote it down the first time, make sure you write it down again.

Reflecting on your feelings before and after you practice gratitude will immediately show you how it changes your thoughts and feelings. Imagine the effect it can have on you in the long term.

Activity Four: Gratitude Buddy

Having someone keep us accountable is one of the best ways to make sure we keep up the good work. Having a gratitude buddy means exactly that: someone who will check in on you and help you on your journey. It's not a one-way relationship, though. You should be doing the same for them.

Choose someone whom you either already have a close relationship with or a relationship that you feel might need some work and you would like to improve it. Share your gratitude entries with your buddy daily and ask them to do the same. It might feel strange initially, perhaps a bit silly, but keep at it. Make notes of any changes in your relationship with your gratitude buddy, whether it's your perception of them or the essence of your relationship.

It doesn't have to be a sit-down conversation. It doesn't even have to be a call. It can be a quick text or a photo. But make sure you both engage with the other person's entry to really derive meaning from this activity.

Sharing what we are grateful for with others not only forces us to do the exercise but also helps us to share things that are close to our hearts. Sharing is one of the best ways to improve a relationship. By sharing your gratitude entries with your buddy, and vice versa, you will definitely inspire each other to keep going.

THE CONNECTION BETWEEN GRATITUDE, HAPPINESS, AND SUCCESS

We've briefly discussed that gratitude can actually lift our moods and help us have a more positive outlook on life. There have been many studies done over the years, and they all have one thing in common: the results support the fact that there is a link between gratitude and improved overall happiness.

One of the most well-known studies on gratitude was done by Emmons and McCullough (2003). There were a total of 192 individuals in the study, which were split into three groups. Each group was given various different assignments to do.

For one particular writing assignment, two of the groups were tasked with something completely random that had no connection to being grateful or thankful, while the last group was specifically tasked to write down five things that they are grateful for in their lives.

The result of the study was that the group of individuals who were forced to reflect on things they were grateful for were, on average, 10% happier than those in the other groups who weren't guided toward gratitude (Emmons & McCullough, 2003).

I understand that it can be difficult to relate to an academic study that was done, so let's look at a few examples where this idea is demonstrated:

- **Appreciating a person:** When we express gratitude toward someone else, it not only makes us happy but also makes the other person happy. Whenever I tell my mom I love and appreciate her, a big smile spreads across her face. Just seeing that makes me automatically feel happier as well.

- **Going down memory lane:** To me, nostalgia is one of the most prominent ways we experience gratitude.

  ○ I think the first example that comes to mind is photos. Looking back at old photos has this way of bringing a smile to my face and a feeling of happiness because it takes me back to that moment. This is why we take photos—in an attempt to capture a moment that makes us feel happy and thankful so that we can remember it later.
  ○ Having a memory journal where every memory, big or small, is recorded is another way to be able to go back and reflect on something that made us happy.
  ○ What I also like to do is keep a box of souvenirs. I think most of us do that to some extent. We keep the movie ticket from the first date we had, the chocolate wrapper from Valentine's Day, or even the bus ticket from that one time your crush sat next to you on the bus. It doesn't matter what it is. Whenever we go through that box again, we're reminded of that moment, and it makes us feel all happy again.

Thinking about all these things, I'm sure it makes a lot more sense now why your mom kept all those drawings from when you were a baby, huh?

You'll notice that these are simple and easy ways to feel happier daily. There are no hoops we need to jump through or a goal we need to reach before we can translate our gratitude into happiness and vice versa.

I see it often when someone expresses dissatisfaction with their lives and tells me that if only things were better, they would be so much happier. If only they did better at school, understood difficult concepts, or were able to learn like their peers. If only they were more successful, then they would be happy.

What most of us seem to miss is that we shouldn't wait to be successful to be happy. We should create our own happiness, and success will follow. The key to success is to start with gratitude. The more gratitude we have, the happier we are, and the more likely we will be to achieve our goals.

When we are happy, we feel more motivated to push harder. The more motivated we are, the more work we put in to reach our goals. Once we achieve them, we are even happier, which leads to increased motivation to set and reach new goals. It's one of the most beautiful and effective loops. That's exactly where you want to be!

What better way to explore gratitude and happiness than looking at people who are successful, listening to uplifting music, and exploring the mind of one of our role models?

Activity Five: Success Stories

A success story is exactly what the name suggests: A situation where we were successful in something. We all have some success stories where things just went our way. Stories where we were the hero or managed to pull something off, no one, or even just ourselves, believed we could.

Take some time to think back on a situation where things turned out really well, and you were successful in what you set out to do. Try to remember the story in as much detail as possible. Now, go through everything that happened again and try to identify elements to be grateful for in the story.

By reflecting on something we did well, we boost our mood and remind ourselves that we are capable. These elements of gratitude that we notice in our success stories are the ingredients that build success. Knowing what they are helps us to leverage them again to reach our goals.

Activity Six: Create a Playlist

A gratitude playlist is a collection of songs that evoke feelings of gratitude in us, which can be very helpful and powerful when we're having a bad day.

Make a list of songs you know speak about gratitude or help you reflect on things to be grateful for. If you struggle to think of any or were only able to identify a handful, do some research on the topic. Google is quite helpful when it comes to that. Once you have a good list of songs, create a playlist on your app of choice, like Apple Music, Spotify, or even YouTube.

Music has a way of affecting our mood. Certain music will evoke certain emotions and can instantly change the atmosphere. By having a gratitude playlist, we can easily tune into a grateful mindset and boost our mood in no time.

Activity Seven: The Role-Model Exercise

A role model is someone that we look up to because they inspire us. We can easily use their success stories to help build our own.

For this activity, the goal is to find someone who embodies gratitude and then trying to dissect their recipe to success. If someone doesn't come to mind immediately, take some time to think about it. Consider people who have impacted your life, who are always happy and positive, or who are very successful. These are the people who are most likely to practice gratitude, but you may not have noticed that in them before.

Take time to look into their success and reflect on it. Write down some of the qualities they have that you admire about them. Find out what is important to them and how they define success. If they're someone you know personally, set up some time to chat to them! I'm sure they would be more than happy to share it with you.

Once you have these aspects and qualities, reflect on ways you can bring some of those aspects and qualities into your own life. Identify any kind of support you might need and use this information to set new goals for yourself.

Having a real-life example of what gratitude can do will change your perspective completely. This exercise should help you realize that gratitude really does lead to success, and as long as we focus and work on the good, better will follow.

CHAPTER 1 SUMMARY

- Gratitude is a feeling of appreciation for something given to us by someone or something other than ourselves.
- Expressing gratitude can make all the difference and help us not take things for granted.
- There is scientific evidence that supports the correlation between gratitude and improved emotional, mental, and physical well-being.
- Gratitude is more important than we realize. It's such a powerful tool that can enhance emotional, mental, and physical well-being and is directly connected to happiness and success.

In the next chapter, we will examine what it takes to adopt a gratitude mindset and how we can shift our perspective to embrace it. We will look at how we can reframe some of our negative thoughts into something more positive and what role mindfulness can play in all of this.

SHIFTING PERSPECTIVES

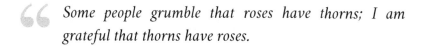

Some people grumble that roses have thorns; I am grateful that thorns have roses.

— ALPHONSE KARR

At times, it may be hard to find something to be grateful for. If you are a teenager living in your parent's house with no job, no money to buy what you want, no friends, and no car to go anywhere, it can be challenging to just be positive and grateful. I get it. In a world that is very focused on instant gratification and having the best of everything, it's easy to feel like there is nothing to be grateful for.

I felt like the quote at the beginning of this chapter just says it so beautifully. If you focus on the thorns, you might not enjoy the roses, regardless of how breathtaking they might be. Accepting that the thorns are part of it and shifting focus to the roses changes the picture completely. It could have been a stalk with thorns, but instead, it also has a rose. How magnificent!

There's this beautiful picture going around where there are two people on a bus. The one that's sitting on the left side of the bus seems sad. You can see from his demeanor that he's not having a good day, and it seems like he's carrying the world's weight on his shoulders. Evidently, when you look out the window on the left side, there is nothing but darkness. Everything is gray and miserable, just like his mood.

The man on the other side of the bus has the biggest smile on his face. He looks really happy and has some binoculars to take in the view. When you look out of the windows on the right side of the bus, there's a lot of greenery, mountains, the sun, and a river that flows through. It's absolutely beautiful.

Both men are on the same bus and have the same opportunities, but they're having completely opposite experiences. If you could chat with the man on the left, where everything is miserable, he would probably tell you that he's having the worst day of his life and he never wants to get on this bus again. You would hear quite the opposite from the other man.

What I'm trying to illustrate here is that what you experience is all based on perspective. And perspective is a choice you can make. You can choose to focus on the positives and sit on the right side of the bus, or you can choose to focus on the negative, sit on the left side of the bus, and disregard whatever is happening on the right.

EXPLORING THE MINDSET SHIFT TO EMBRACE GRATITUDE

Gratitude is more than just a feeling. It's more than just feeling appreciative of something. To really embrace gratitude, there needs to be an attitude and mindset shift. That means that we choose to see the good amid a storm. Having an attitude full of gratitude can reshape our outlook on life to always see the good.

There's an interesting concept that Elizabeth Bostwick (2020) touches on in her article on gratitude. Every day, we have an opportunity to embrace what we get to do on that particular day. Most of us choose to focus on it as something that we have to do, especially if we don't particularly enjoy the task. What she is suggesting is reframing that thought and seeing it as something that we get to do.

For example, when the task is to do your homework. Instead of seeing it as something that you need to do, think about it differently. You are very privileged to be in a school where they're trying to further your understanding. Being educated is one of the most important aspects of our world today. Without education, we can't do anything. Thousands of children across the world don't have that privilege. They either can't afford it, or their country is not set up for it. Receiving education is definitely something to be grateful for.

It may be difficult at first to feel grateful, but try to see it through a different lens. Those children will give anything to be the ones to have to do homework.

Maybe it's hard to relate to that if you haven't really seen the impact that no education has on someone's life. The primary providers of these families are forced to work more than one job just to provide the bare minimum for their families because they earn minimum wage. It's not their fault, and if they could, they would change it in an instant. Most of them become immigrants in other countries, legal or not, just to try and make a living.

While your mom might make something for dinner that you don't really like, another child wishes that their mom was still around to make them dinner, regardless of what she makes.

The aim of this book is not to bring you down or make you worry about these families, but it's important to reflect on how lucky and privileged we are to have these things in our lives. Things that we take for granted.

Sometimes, we lose perspective on what we should be thankful for because we take it for granted. What's supposed to be a blessing to us becomes something that we can easily complain about. The challenge is to identify these and start seeing them as blessings again. I promise you that it will make such a big difference. It's not going to be a small difference that manifests over time. You will see the change in your mood and attitude immediately.

I have some really interesting activities lined up for this one. It will help to start the work on shifting our perspective.

Activity Eight: Reframe the Day

An ordinary day of running errands always has something in it to be grateful for. But what about a challenging day? There's always something, even on your worst day. We might just need to look a little harder for something to be grateful for.

Think about a particularly challenging day. You know the one —the day where everything seems to go wrong, you do every-thing wrong, and at the end of the day, you feel completely drained. Or just a day you feel was a really bad day, no explana-tion needed. It was bad from the moment you woke up until it was finally time for bed, and you were hoping that the next day would be better.

Now, what I want you to do with this day in mind is to reflect on everything that happened and find at least three aspects of the day for which you can express gratitude. Write them down so that you remember them the next time you have a difficult day.

By finding some things to be grateful for on our most chal-lenging days, we show ourselves that there is always something to be thankful for. Sometimes, we just need to look at things differently and change our perspective.

Activity Nine: Future Self-Letter

This involves writing a letter to our future selves to express gratitude for the difficult times that are still to come and seeing them as life lessons that will lead to self-improvement. It can be difficult to see a storm as a lesson to improve while we are in the midst of it.

The first step to writing a letter to your future self is to make sure that your environment is set up for inspiration. Use whatever makes you feel relaxed, calm, and optimistic to get into the right frame of mind. There is no right or wrong when it comes to the content of the letter, as long as it's uplifting and touches on gratitude for every situation. If you are not sure what to include, here are some pointers:

- Start with the reason you are writing the letter.
- Tell them how you are feeling right now.
- Tell them about the journey you've embarked on to be more grateful.
- Talk about your dreams and aspirations for the future.
- Cover what gratitude means to you and why it's important to always focus on gratitude.

This form of self-reflection results in immeasurable personal growth and helps with keeping our minds on things that are bigger than our current circumstances. It helps us to acknowledge that there will be trials and tribulations but also that we're ready to learn from them to be a better version of ourselves. The best time to read this letter is every single time you go through a difficult season. It could be in a week's time, maybe a year, or even several years from now.

Activity Ten: Gratitude Board

A gratitude board is like a vision board; however, instead of just covering our aspirations and goals, the aim of a gratitude board is to showcase anything that inspires gratitude. This can be photos, pictures, quotes, books, or anything else that makes us feel grateful.

How you want to make your gratitude board is completely up to you. Everyone's board will look different, and that's okay. Yours is not supposed to look exactly the same as mine because each board needs to inspire its maker. The first step is to decide what kind of gratitude board you want to make. Here are some inspirational ideas to get you started, but remember that it can be anything you want it to be. It can be a big placard filled with:

- quotes on gratitude.
- pictures that inspire gratitude.
- drawings.
- letters from those we love.
- a combination of some or all of these.

It's really one of my favorite activities because there's no limit to the creativity that can go into this. Creating it and being able to look at it daily will really help to get you through some of the toughest days. And remember, you can always add more to it. Just because you already made it doesn't mean you can't change it up every now and then.

REFRAMING NEGATIVE THOUGHTS

An essential part of cultivating a gratitude mindset is reframing negative thoughts into more positive ones. It's normal to feel overwhelmed or anxious sometimes, but when we set up camp with those emotions, they can do a lot more harm than good.

How we think influences how we feel, and how we feel and think influences our actions. If our thinking is negative, our feelings will be negative, and we will behave based on that. Our behavior then influences what we think, and so on. It's nearly impossible to express gratitude when we're caught in this cycle of unhelpful thoughts.

Let's look at some of the most common negative thoughts and the best ways to reframe them with a positive spin.

▷ **All-Or-Nothing Thinking**

This is for everyone who thinks in black and white—who believes that something is either right or wrong. They don't believe in gray areas. If education is important to them, they need to get a distinction for every subject; otherwise, they believe that they did poorly. It's a very difficult mindset to live up to. We always need to make space for gray areas.

Reframing this can be difficult. It's important to surround yourself with people who believe in you. In these moments, you need to remember that no one is perfect. We are all human, which means we can all make mistakes. You allow others to live in the gray areas, and you support them no matter what. Why can't you do the same? Be kind to yourself next time this happens. It's okay to not be perfect.

▷ Predicting the Future

I think we have all been guilty of this one. We think we already know what's going to happen, what someone is going to say, or how they are going to react. This may lead to us going down the rabbit hole of negative thoughts without anything even happening yet.

Instead of expecting the worst next time, expect the best. Imagine the best-case scenario playing out instead. The more positivity you put into the situation, the bigger the chance is of having a positive outcome.

▷ Putting Everything Under a Magnifying Glass

This is a very common distortion that most people struggle with. It's when something happens, or someone says something, and without any further information (or any evidence of it), and we make the worst unjustified conclusion. Making a bigger deal of something than it actually is and then justifying it based on the conclusions we made ourselves. It's a very toxic mindset that can spiral out of control very quickly.

Whenever you are having these thoughts, try to pinpoint where they are coming from and why you are drawing those specific conclusions. Dealing with the root of the issue is very important to prevent this from happening again. Show yourself that there is no evidence of the worst case scenario. Think about the future and set some goals in relation to that specific issue. For example, when one of my students failed a test, they told me that they weren't smart enough. There was no evidence to support that because they were doing well in every other subject. We reframed those thoughts by setting a goal for her to get a distinction for the same subject by the end of the school year.

▷ Making It Personal

Everything is our fault, whether we had a hand in it or not. When we have this kind of thinking, we believe that everything that happens around us is somehow our fault or involves us. For example, when people are giggling close by, we assume that they are laughing at us when, in reality, someone probably told a joke they heard at a party last night.

When this happens, you need to try to put things back into perspective. Just because you are in the vicinity when something happens doesn't mean that it has anything to do with you. Just focus on yourself and stop worrying about everyone around you.

▷ Stewing

This is when we keep running through the same thoughts over and over and reliving the situation that caused it. Doing this keeps us in a negative mindset, and we struggle to notice the positives.

Being able to immediately identify that we are having these thoughts is the first step to reframing them. As soon as we identify it, we need to put a stop to it and replace it with something else. A good way to do this is to always have a list of things on hand that make us happy so that we can refer to it whenever we need to.

The activities in this chapter are dedicated to improving our thinking patterns and preventing negative thoughts from taking over.

Activity Eleven: The Flip Side

It's always important to look at the flip side, and this activity is going to help you do it. Looking at the flip side involves reframing a negative thought into something more positive or neutral.

Start by writing down some of the most common negative thoughts you often have. Those thoughts really get the best of you and make you expect the worst. Leave some space after each one for the flip side.

Once you've made a list, reframe those thoughts by flipping it into something that's more positive or even neutral. I have included some examples below.

Negative thought	The flip side
"I'm too scared to try this. It will be my first time. I don't know whether I can do it."	"This is such a great learning opportunity to grow my skills."
"I don't have the money/time to do this."	"How can I make this work?"
"It's too hard."	"Let me try and look at this from a different angle."
"It's pointless. I've already tried five times. I give up."	"Let me try again." Remember, you only fail when you stop trying.
"No one wants to be my friend."	"What can I do differently to make more friends?"

By looking at the flip side, we create opportunities for ourselves instead of feeling like we've hit a brick wall. It's an excellent way to identify areas where we can better ourselves.

Activity Twelve: Positivity Jar

I love this activity! Not that I don't love all of them, but this is definitely another favorite for me. A positivity jar is a jar full of positivity. Sounds simple? It really is.

Find a jar that you can use for this activity. The bigger the jar, the better! We're going to fill it with some positivity. Take a piece of paper and add a note of positivity to the jar every day. This can be for yourself (like, "You look amazing today"), something that happened during the day that made you smile, memories, or even quotes.

The positivity jar will not only help you focus on the positives but can also help you out when you are in a pickle. Whenever you are having a bad day, open your jar of positivity and read some of those notes. It will definitely make you feel better.

Activity Thirteen: Gratitude Reminders

A gratitude reminder forces you to think about something you are grateful for in that moment.

Set a reminder on your phone to have a moment of gratitude sometime during the day. When is your most difficult and stressful part of the day? Maybe try to schedule it before, after, or even during that time so that you are forced to take a moment and just be grateful for something. It will brighten your day and that moment.

We get so caught up in our days sometimes and can easily fall into negative thinking when we're laser-focused. Setting a reminder to be grateful for something is a great way to break out of that and help us put things back into perspective.

THE ROLE OF MINDFULNESS

Mindfulness is one of the best tools that we can use to live in the moment and appreciate what we have. The essence of mindfulness involves completely focusing on the now with a clear vision, no agenda, and no judgment. When mindful, we are more likely to identify aspects to be grateful for. Mindfulness is an excellent base for cultivating gratitude.

Living in the moment can really help us to identify things to be grateful for. For example, if we just take a walk to the shop and focus on getting there, then all we did was take a walk to the shop. If we practice mindfulness while walking, we might notice a few interesting things along the way, which could turn into a mindful gratitude walk.

Mindfulness also ensures that we don't do things out of habit in the sense that they don't mean anything. When we link mindfulness to gratitude, we can be sure that our appreciation always has meaning behind it.

These activities are all about being mindful while expressing gratitude. It will really help to bring the two together.

Activity Fourteen: Mindful Eating

I feel like, most times, we just eat for the sake of eating. We eat because we're hungry or because someone offered us food. When last did you really sit back and enjoy every single part of the eating experience? I'm not talking just about the taste of the food. Mindful eating involves a few different aspects. It touches on what we choose to eat, why we eat it, how much we eat, and how we eat it.

Next time you are enjoying a meal, make it a mindful experience. Here are some pointers to help you:

- **Honor the food:** It's important to acknowledge where the meal came from. Did someone prepare it in your house? Is it at a restaurant? Where did the ingredients come from? Really think about the people who harvested those ingredients, those who went out to purchase the ingredients, and those who prepared the meal. Take a moment to appreciate this process.
- **Use all your senses:** Most of the time, we only engage smell and taste when we eat. What about the other sense? Use all of them to make it a meaningful experience and appreciate the meal from a different angle. Listen for any sounds that may come from eating the meal, such as crunch. See the colors in the meal, smell each ingredient, and appreciate the different textures in the meal. Take a moment to enjoy every aspect of the meal.

- **Take smaller bites and eat slowly:** Instead of gulping it all down because it's so good, take smaller bites. Chew the food thoroughly before swallowing, and pause for a moment before you take the next bite. This will also help to prevent overeating.

Mindful eating will give you a whole new appreciation for food and help to prevent binge eating.

Activity Fifteen: Read Gratitude Quotes

Gratitude quotes are nicely strung-together words that were said by someone else. We don't have to reinvent the wheel here. Someone already said it better than we might be able to.

Research some gratitude quotes and write them down for future use. There are thousands to be found, and I'm positive that you will find quite a few that resonate with you. There is one at the beginning of each chapter in this book to get you started. Take some time to reflect on these quotes and really try to unpack what the author was trying to get across. See how you can apply it to your life.

Someone already put what we're thinking into words and made a quote out of it. They were able to state it beautifully for everyone else to enjoy. Reading these quotes can be so motivational and help to propel us forward and strive for more.

Activity Sixteen: Positive Self-Talk

We talk to ourselves all day, every day. We are the person that we spend the most time with. Why can't we always be kind to ourselves? Positive self-talk focuses on being kind to ourselves and letting the inner us know that we are doing a good job at life.

You can do this in the mirror. In fact, I encourage you to. It's most effective that way, even if it feels silly in the beginning. Use gratitude affirmations to turn your talk into positive self-talk. Here are some examples:

- I am so grateful that I have a voice.
- I am grateful for my beautiful eyes.
- I am grateful because I can think and speak.
- I am grateful for my mind.
- I am grateful because I am unique.
- I am grateful for the talents that I have (you can list your talents in the affirmation).
- I am grateful for my ability to draw people in.

These are mostly surface-level, but don't be afraid to go deeper. These are just to get you started. Use your strengths to talk yourself up. By doing this, you create a more positive self-image, which will not only boost your confidence but also help you to see the good around you. You attract what you focus on. Focusing on the good in you will attract more good toward you.

CHAPTER 2 SUMMARY

- We need to change our mindset to embrace gratitude rather than just thinking about it. Changing our attitude, not just our feelings, will help us get to where we want to be.
- It's easy to get captivated by negative thoughts. As soon as they crop up, we need to reframe them into something more positive or neutral. Instead of creating problems, we open up possibilities for ourselves.
- Mindfulness is a core pillar of gratitude because it helps us to focus on the present and not worry about anything else.

Completing the activities in this chapter has helped to lay a solid foundation for embracing gratitude and reframing negative thoughts. In the next chapter, we will discuss emotional well-being, increasing self-esteem, and reducing stress.

GRATITUDE AND EMOTIONAL WELL-BEING

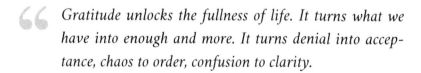

Gratitude unlocks the fullness of life. It turns what we have into enough and more. It turns denial into acceptance, chaos to order, confusion to clarity.

— MELODY BEATTIE

This quote is so appropriate for me because although it also deals with perspective, it delivers the essence of gratitude and the link with emotional well-being so well. When we practice gratitude, focusing on the good is easier, which turns our emotions into positive ones.

We've all had a bad day before, and we've looked at how gratitude can improve our mood. But, what about depression and anxiety? These are chronic conditions that some of us have to live with.

These conditions can have a snowball effect on our self-esteem, self-image, and productivity. It can also increase our stress levels and make us feel like we're drowning. In some instances, we may need medication to help us cope.

If you have been formally diagnosed with a mental condition, please note that this is not medical advice, and you should always consult with your treating provider before you make any changes to your treatment. However, it has been scientifically proven that a gratitude mindset can improve the symptoms and help those living with these conditions lead more fulfilling lives.

HOW GRATITUDE HELPS WITH DEPRESSION AND ANXIETY

Not all of us experience depression and anxiety in the same way or to the same degree. For some, it might be an off day every now and then, while others have to take medication every day just to be okay. It doesn't matter where you fall on this spectrum. There is one commonality across the spectrum: negative thinking patterns. We experience these emotions because we focus on everything that has gone wrong in the past or everything we expect to go wrong in the future. By dwelling on these things, we get more worried, which causes the release of cortisol, the stress hormone.

Increased cortisol can lead to a decrease in serotonin, which is one of the hormones that make us feel happy. How do we combat that? With gratitude, of course. We already discussed in

Chapter 1 that practicing gratitude increases the release of dopamine and serotonin.

Practicing gratitude and finding something to be grateful for is most powerful when we're at a very low point. That's exactly when we should look for reasons to be grateful. The more things we can find to be happy about, the more dopamine and serotonin our brains will release and the happier we will feel. The opposite is also true: The more we dwell on the negative, the more cortisol our brain will release and the more depressed or anxious we will feel.

Gratitude is not a magical cure that will take depression and anxiety away forever, but it is a very powerful tool that we can use to manage the symptoms of those conditions and improve our overall mental well-being.

There is only one activity for this section to help us gain control of our emotions and focus on gratitude.

Activity Seventeen: Gratitude Meditation

To meditate simply means to focus your energy and become aware of your current state in an attempt to organize thoughts and reach a calm state of mind. There are many techniques that one can use to meditate, including gratitude. Gratitude meditation can be practiced daily. It doesn't have to be a lengthy exercise. Meditating for only 15 minutes a day is more than enough to reap the benefits.

To start with the meditation, make sure you are wearing comfortable clothes and find a quiet place where you won't be disturbed. You can choose to either sit upright or lie down on your back with a pillow under your knees for optimal comfort. Make sure that you are comfortable. If you are feeling uncomfortable, it will affect your meditation. If the room is a little cold, put on a sweater or use a blanket to stay nice and toasty.

When you are ready, close your eyes and slowly take a deep breath that reaches into your belly, and then breathe out. Focus on letting go of anything that is stressing you out. Imagine that you are breathing all that toxicity out. If you need to take a second breath, that's okay. Once you are ready, you can move on to the next part.

Mentally scan your body to identify any tension that you might be carrying somewhere—anywhere your muscles might feel a little tense or painful. As you take the next breath in, imagine channeling it to those places and the air grabbing it and pulling it out as you breathe out again. Spend about a minute or two on this to make sure that you get rid of all the tension and pain.

Next, focus on any negative feelings you may have. Things like jealousy, anxiety, anger, or even judgment. Take a deep breath in, acknowledge these feelings, and then remove them as you slowly breathe out.

The last step to help get to a state of peace is to identify any plans, thoughts, ideas, or anything else in your mind that does not relate to the meditation. Take another deep breath in and breathe them out as you exhale.

If you followed these steps correctly, you should be in a state of clarity and peace because there is nothing you are holding on to at this point. This creates the perfect opportunity to fill the empty canvas with gratitude.

There are so many things to be grateful for. Here are some points to help you with the meditation:

- You can start with the fact that you are alive and have made it to this point.
- You were taught how to do various things, including talk, walk, eat by yourself, understand, and everything else that makes you human.
- Your heart is beating and pumping blood to the rest of your body to keep you alive.
- Take a moment to reflect on how amazing your body is: how it knows exactly what to do and when to do it. Appreciate what a well-oiled machine it is.
- You can also reflect on how privileged we are to live in the world we do today.

  ○ We have electricity, running water, televisions, internet, cellphones, vehicles, and so many other things that generations before us may not have had. We are exceptionally fortunate to have access to all these things.

- We don't have to hunt for meat or forage for food. We can simply go to the supermarket and buy something to eat.
- Think about the people and pets that you have in your life—those that have a direct impact on your life. Think

about how they support you, make you laugh, and make you feel wanted and appreciated.

- Remember to also reflect on anything else that you are grateful for and allow that to fill your mind, body, and heart.

Spend some time in this state and just enjoy the feeling. Notice how your body is feeling and the thoughts that are running through your mind. When you are ready, you can get up and continue with your day.

The more you do this, the easier it will become. The first few times might feel a little weird or like you are not doing it right, but keep persisting.

Gratitude meditation can help to put things back in perspective and help to let go of anything negative that is dragging us down. It's an excellent way to press the reset button.

INCREASE SELF-ESTEEM AND DEVELOPING POSITIVE SELF-IMAGE

Our self-image is how we see ourselves and dynamically changes over the years. Many factors can influence our self-image, including accomplishments, failures, strengths, and weaknesses.

The self-image we have influences how we respond in certain situations. For example, someone who believes they are a people person will be able to speak to others with ease. However, if they believe they are shy, it won't come as easy.

We can perceive the image we see when we look in the mirror as either positive or negative. Having a positive self-image does not mean that we think we're perfect but rather that we accept our areas of development and choose to focus on our strengths —everything that makes us great.

More often than not, we easily see the good in others, but we're our own worst critic. Learning to be kind to ourselves is so important. I know that it may be difficult if those around you are constantly bringing you down. If you do experience that often, there are two options: either a chat needs to be had with those people (if possible), or you need to distance yourself from them. Those who can't even see the good in others don't deserve to be part of your life.

When you think of some of the happiest times in your life, can you identify anything all those events have in common? I bet something happened or someone did something that made you feel grateful and happy, which helps with a positive self-image. It's clear that there is a direct link between practicing gratitude and having a positive self-image. The more gratitude you express, the more you realize what you have to be grateful for, and the better your self-image will be.

With social media and what they portray as perfect, it can be difficult to believe in our own superpowers. But they are there; we just need to identify and showcase them!

Let's look at some activities that can help us with this.

Activity Eighteen: Affirmations

Affirmations are amazing in building a positive self-image. For this activity, we want to focus on self-gratitude to help build confidence as well as practice gratitude. Two birds with one stone!

Get a pen and paper ready. We want to write down as many gratitude affirmations as we can. An affirmation normally starts with "I am." In this case, those words should be followed with the word grateful. Think of all the things you take for granted that you should feel grateful for. Those things that either make life possible or make your life more bearable. Here are a few examples:

- I am grateful for the people in my life.
- I am grateful for the clothes I wear.
- I am grateful for the food I eat every day.
- I am grateful that I have a lovely home.
- I am grateful for my parents.
- I am grateful for my pets.
- I am grateful that I get to experience the beauty of life every day.
- I am grateful to be in good health.
- I am grateful that I am me.

You get the idea. Once you have your list of self-gratitude affirmations, make some time to read them every morning when you wake up. Your day will start differently, and you will feel more grateful as the day goes on.

Gratitude affirmations are a great way to remind ourselves of our daily blessings, and they definitely help to form a more positive self-image. Why should we be unhappy if there are so many things to be grateful for?

Activity Nineteen: Mirror Exercise

I know a lot of people are not a fan of these mirror exercises because they don't like looking at themselves in the mirror. Why not? Because they don't always like what they see. And that's exactly what we want to change here.

This mirror exercise is to practice appreciation for the person staring back at us. Once we can start appreciating that person, a positive self-image will follow easily. It might feel weird in the beginning, maybe even silly. But it works. Just keep at it. How you decide to do it is completely up to you. But for those who are not too familiar with the process, here are a few tips to get started.

All you need is a mirror and a few minutes to spend in front of it. Start with five minutes a day where you just stare at your own face in the mirror and repeat positive affirmations about yourself. Things like "I am beautiful and kind," or "I love myself," or even "I am good enough" are all gold. You can start with either physical attributes or characteristics, but make sure that you cover both in the five minutes. After a week or two, increase the time to ten minutes a day. As you get more comfortable, increase how much you see of yourself in the mirror, i.e., start complimenting your whole body instead of just your face.

By doing this mirror exercise, we are helping ourselves to overcome any insecurities we have, improve our self-esteem, boost confidence, and connect to our inner child. It's such a powerful exercise that I still practice daily.

Activity Twenty: One Day of Gratitude

Imagine a whole day where we just focus on the positive. That's what this activity is all about. We are going to have a whole day where we only focus on the positive.

From the second you wake up, fill your mind and your speech with positive language. Don't press the snooze button or think *Just five more minutes, Mom!* Get up, get dressed, and get ready to have the best day! Focus on everything that is good. If something upsets you, either change your perspective on the situation or disregard it completely. There's no space for negativity today.

We already know how powerful it is to focus on the positive, so let's put it into action.

Activity Twenty-One: Body Scan

For this activity, we're going to tap into our meditation techniques again but instead of just being mindful, we're going to actually thank our bodies for doing the work to keep us alive and thriving.

Make sure that you are in a comfortable position, either sitting up straight or lying down. You can close your eyes if you want to. Take a few deep breaths in and out just to get completely focused on the present moment. Once you are ready, start scanning your body from the top down. The whole point of the exercise is to express thanks to the various parts of your body for the way they support you. How you choose to thank them is completely up to you. Here is an example: When focusing on your head, thank:

- your brain for doing all the hard work.
- your eyes for seeing the beauty life has to offer.
- your tongue for helping you experience exquisite cuisine.
- your nose for helping you smell the flowers (and the role it plays in eating).
- you ears for hearing all the beautiful sounds, like the birds chirping.

However you choose to thank those parts of your body, make sure that you are specific and that you cover them all before you move on to the next part of your body.

This will give us a new appreciation of our bodies and what they do for us daily. It helps us to really connect with our bodies and reach a new level of gratitude.

GRATITUDE AND STRESS REDUCTION

Some people have a natural gift to deal better with life's struggles. Or maybe it has crossed your mind that nothing is ever that bad for them. That's what it seems like from the outside, anyway. The truth? Everyone has that ability–it just takes a little bit of work on our part to cultivate it.

Earlier in the chapter, we already established that gratitude decreases the stress hormone in our bodies, which significantly decreases the feelings of stress. Our stress hormone is cortisol. The more cortisol we release, the more stressed we feel. The more stressed we feel, the more cortisol we release. It is a vicious cycle that needs to be avoided or broken at best.

Practicing gratitude daily can help us to get a hold of stress and live a happier life where we feel calm and in control.

The two activities included in this section have been specifically chosen to help with those stress levels and manage them better. Remember these whenever you are feeling a little overwhelmed.

Activity Twenty-Two: Stress-Gratitude Log

If you feel stressed most days, this is a great way to start turning it around and finding things to be grateful for during stressful situations.

Get a journal or a book (and a pen) that you can carry everywhere you go. Whenever something happens that puts stress on you or you feel anxious about something, journal it down in as much detail as possible. Once done, find things you can be grateful for in the scenario. You can even do the reflection at night after the day is over.

By making it a point to reflect and find things to be grateful for, even in stressful situations, you teach your mind not to go into fight-or-flight mode as soon as something goes wrong.

Activity Twenty-Three: Gratitude Breathing

This exercise may be similar to meditation, and you can choose to do the two interchangeably (i.e., not do both on the same day). I still wanted to include this exercise as it's really powerful. During the breathing exercises, we allow the gratitude thought to spread to the rest of our bodies.

Similar to what we do for meditation, find a spot where you are comfortable and won't be disturbed. For these breathing exercises, make sure that your feet are on the floor. Inhale and exhale in any way you like, focusing on releasing any tension in your body. If you feel the need to stretch your back, neck, arms, and legs to release more tension, do it. The more relaxed you feel, the better.

When you are ready, take a deep breath in through your nose, counting to six. We're going to focus on a few things here as we breathe in:

- Imagine your heart is receiving all of it and expanding as you breathe in.
- To have an even better experience, put your one hand over your heart while you do this.
- Think about something you are grateful for and say it in your mind. For example, I am grateful for my cat.

While you hold onto that gratitude thought, breathe out for six counts, allowing the gratitude you just felt in your heart to flow through the rest of your body. You can continue with this exercise until you feel calm, relaxed, and ready to take on the rest of the day.

This exercise really helps us to feel centered and refocus on what is important, which is everything that makes us feel good, happy, and grateful.

CHAPTER 3 SUMMARY

- Gratitude is a great tool in managing symptoms of anxiety and depression.
- We can also improve our self-image and boost our self-esteem by practicing gratitude daily.
- Because of the hormones we release when practicing gratitude, it's also an amazing way to reduce stress and build greater resilience.

Gratitude significantly improves our mental health, reduces symptoms of anxiety and depression, and promotes self-esteem. This all can lead to better relationships with those around us. In the next chapter, we explore how gratitude can change the connection we have with others to build a solid foundation.

NURTURING RELATIONSHIPS

Let us be grateful to the people who make us happy; they are the charming gardeners who make our souls blossom.

— MARCEL PROUST

I definitely could not have said this better myself. As humans, we are programmed to engage in fellowship. We want to be around people (even if it's just one other person) and we need relationships. There are so many books and motivational speakers that tell us what the important pillars of building effective relationships are. You will find that most of them mention appreciating the other person and not taking anything for granted.

We tend to forget that sometimes, which is why it's become increasingly difficult to maintain relationships and even build new ones. It's easier for us to just continue living our lives and only worry about what we need to do. The only time that we acknowledge others is when we take stock of what they're bringing to the table. If it's not enough, or we feel like we bring more, we distance ourselves even more without thinking that we may have had a hand in the relationship going downhill.

This is not only applicable to romantic relationships but also relationships with your family, friends, peers, and work colleagues (once you have a job). All relationships need work, and gratitude is a big part of it.

In this chapter, we'll look at why it's so important to express gratitude in relationships, how it cultivates amazing relationships, and some tips on how to express sincere gratitude toward others. Gratitude really is the cheat sheet when it comes to just about anything good in life. When we start living a life of gratitude, it's much easier to make those around us feel appreciated because it becomes a way of life.

IMPORTANCE OF EXPRESSING GRATITUDE IN RELATIONSHIPS

Whether your love language is words of affirmation or not, it's always nice to know that you are appreciated and that others like it a bit more when you are around. A simple but sincere "thank you" or "I appreciate you" can make a huge difference in a relationship. Sometimes, it's all we need to hear to know everything is still on track.

Has that ever happened to you? Have you ever had an argument with someone close to you that resulted in you not speaking to them for a couple of days? And then they suddenly reach out and tell you that they appreciate you, or any version of it that expresses gratitude. Or maybe you've been on the other end, where you were the one reaching out to let the other know that your life is better because they are a part of it. How did that make you feel? Whether you give or receive gratitude in a relationship, both can be very powerful. Ideally, both people should be expressing gratitude toward the other to make things work.

Here are some reasons why gratitude is important in a relationship and why it makes such a big difference:

- By showing gratitude, we let the other person know that they have done something good, which makes them feel valued.
- Gratitude celebrates the positives and helps everyone involved to feel closer.
- It shows the other person that you care and that there's something in them that you admire.
- Feeling grateful for something is one thing. When you express that gratitude, it's felt between both parties and strengthens the bond.
- Expressing gratitude also makes us happy in the relationship and creates room for great things to happen.

When we feel valued and appreciated, we want to stick around and make the other person feel the same way. We are also more inclined to do good to those who we appreciate and who appreciate us.

Here is a fun activity to practice this.

Activity Twenty-Four: Daily Appreciation

Telling someone often that we appreciate them can turn any bad day into a good one, not just for them but for us too! We've already seen what an amazing effect gratitude has on our overall well-being and attitude. What if you expressed gratitude toward someone every day? That's what this activity is all about.

Whether it's someone in your household, a friend, a teacher, extended family, or the person at the grocery store who helps you with check out, tell someone something that you appreciate about them. Tell them how what they do makes a difference to you. Challenge yourself to choose someone new to express gratitude to every day. If you really want to be an overachiever, tell more than one person.

By showing gratitude, you will strengthen existing bonds and form new ones. The power of gratitude should not be underestimated, especially when it comes to relationships. Don't be surprised when you find yourself in a position where it's difficult to choose a bestie to spend all your time with.

HOW GRATITUDE FOSTERS EMPATHY

Before we get into it, let's quickly define what empathy means.

Empathy is the ability to see a situation from someone else's perspective. To walk a mile in their shoes, as some would say it. What's important about empathy is that you need to remember to take off your shoes first before you put theirs on. Most of the time, we try to see things from someone else's perspective and understand their feelings about it, but we still try to do it through our own lens.

One person might drop their ice cream, and that will be the worst thing to happen to them, while another has nothing warm to wear on a cold day. For the person without a jacket, the fact that someone dropped their ice cream seems like a minor issue compared to their issue. Empathy is the ability to understand that whatever that person is going through is tough for them based on their current circumstances.

Just like empathy, gratitude has a lot to do with perspective and what we choose to focus on. Expressing gratitude helps us to see things from a different perspective, which is exactly what empathy is all about. This is why practicing gratitude can help us cultivate better empathy for others. Here are two activities to get started.

Activity Twenty-Five: Kindness Jar

A kindness jar is a jar filled with kindness! It's a jar that helps you reminisce on some of the small acts of kindness that you may have experienced or witnessed. It's also a great way to reflect.

Get a jar or any other container that you want to keep your kindness in. Whenever you experience acts of kindness, write it down and place it in the container. Try to find something every day, even if you aren't on the receiving end.

By focusing on acts of kindness, it's easier for us to see the good in the world. A kindness jar helps to boost our spirit when we need it and guides us toward reflection.

Activity Twenty-Six: Giving to Others

This is quite a simple one: Giving something to others in need. Whether it's time or resources, we all have something we can give.

Find a cause or organization that you are passionate about and reach out to them to find out how you can contribute to helping them. If it's an orphanage or home, you can go through your cupboards and see which clothes you can donate that are still in good condition. Encourage the rest of the family to do the same so that you can take all of it at once. You can even ask your mom whether there are any non-perishable foods that you can donate. If you don't have anything they need, offer a helping hand. Non-profit organizations can always use a helping hand!

If you choose a pet shelter, you can gather pet supplies, food, and blankets for them. Or just offer your time. Pet shelters always need more people to spend time with the animals.

Whatever cause you choose, you can always make a difference. Every little bit helps, and it will not only help them but also enrich your own life.

TIPS FOR EXPRESSING GRATITUDE

There are many ways you can express gratitude toward others, so this is definitely not a complete list. These are just some guidelines to help you get started. I'm sure you'll be able to add a few of your own in no time.

- **Always be respectful:** Being respectful costs us nothing. Whoever it is you are in contact with, always remain respectful. Even if they start screaming and shouting at you. They might be having a bad day. If a family member or friend says something that you don't like, remain respectful. Showing respect at all times shows the other person that you value them and what they bring to the table.
- **Perform random acts of kindness:** Whether it's helping someone you know or a random stranger, random acts of kindness involve doing something nice for someone else without them needing to ask and without wanting something in return. Helping an old lady or man across the street, carrying some grocery bags for a stranger, or leaving a nice note on someone's desk are all examples. Anything kind!
- **Make sure to tip:** If you are out at a restaurant, always tip the server—even if there was something wrong with the food or you waited long. Most of the time it's not

the server's fault. They are doing the best they can and rarely receive gratitude. Be the one to show it.

Although the above can also apply to friends and family, there are some additional ways you can show gratitude toward those closest to you:

- **Just say it:** The simplest way to do it is to say the words. Tell them that you are grateful for them and their existence. Tell them what they did that made you feel grateful. Whatever the reason is that you feel grateful for them, make sure you say those words to them.
- **Write it in a note (or an instant message):** Writing down all the things we appreciate about someone is sure to make them feel all warm and fuzzy inside. It doesn't have to be an entire essay, but write it from the heart. Don't use fancy words or google anything that you can say. Just let your heart express how much you appreciate them.
- **Have a sincere check-in:** We often ask people how they're doing out of habit, without really listening to their response. Similarly, most people respond with "Good, you?" out of habit and not necessarily because they are good. Take some time to have a sincere check-in with the person and find out how they are.
- **Get creative:** Make them something thoughtful. When executed well, a handmade gift can mean the world. Executing something well does not mean that it's perfect. It simply means that you put a lot of thought into it, and it's something that the other person will

value. If it's something they can use regularly, even
better! They'll think about you every time they use it.

The activities below will help put some of these into practice,
but try the rest of them out, too.

Activity Twenty-Seven: Positive Influences

We all have people who have a positive influence in our lives.
They always motivate us to be a better version of ourselves.
Whether it's for physical health, mental health, working on
ourselves, or even just for what we have achieved, these are all
things that we can appreciate.

Take some time to think about all the people in your life who
have had a positive influence on you. It doesn't have to be
current or even recent. Make a list of those people and what
exactly they did that you appreciated.

Realizing who has influenced your life in a positive manner
helps to identify which people to keep close and which relationships to focus on.

Activity Twenty-Eight: Thank You Notes

Now that you have a list of those people, it's time to write some
thank you notes.

Take the list of names you made above and, if possible, express
your gratitude toward them in any way you like. It can be face-

to-face, with a letter, small thank you notes, or even over social media.

Expressing gratitude toward these individuals will let them know that they've made a difference in your life and that you look up to them. It will make them feel good and motivate them to do the same for others. It will also help you to feel more connected with them.

CHAPTER 4 SUMMARY

- We all have a desire to build meaningful relationships with others.
- To build and maintain healthy relationships, we need to express gratitude toward those we appreciate.
- By practicing gratitude, we learn to be more empathetic so that we can relate to others and build strong connections.
- There are many ways we can express gratitude toward others, including saying it, writing a note, having check-ins, and getting creative.

It's clear that expressing gratitude in relationships fosters empathy and compassion and strengthens social connections. In Chapter 5, we will discuss how gratitude can help us overcome challenges.

Thank You

★★★★★

I am writing to express my deepest gratitude for
taking the time to leave a book review.
Your words hold immense value, not only for me as
the author but also for other potential readers
considering purchasing the book.

Your contribution aids fellow readers in making
informed decisions and helps create a community of
thoughtful literary engagement.

Thank you for being a crucial part of this journey,
where your voice amplifies the significance of sharing
stories and knowledge.

Sydney Sheppard

BUILDING RESILIENCE

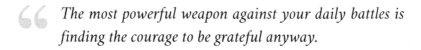 *The most powerful weapon against your daily battles is finding the courage to be grateful anyway.*

— UNKNOWN

L ife isn't always butterflies and roses. Sometimes, we have to face really difficult situations and try our best to overcome them. It's not always easy, and at times, I have felt that I might not make it through this time. But you know what? I always have. I could have dealt with certain things better and gotten through them quicker if I only had the knowledge I have now. I try not to dwell on that because I know I made the best decisions at the time based on the knowledge and resources I had available.

The more we go through challenging times, the more tools we can put in our toolbox for overcoming things, and the better equipped we are for the next time. There will always be a next time. We know that, just like we know, the seasons will change: Summer will turn into autumn, autumn will turn into winter, and so on. There is always more we need to go through. It builds character and forms us into the amazing human beings we are.

Resilience is not something we all automatically have. Most of the time, we build it up over time based on the experiences we go through and the support we receive during those tough times.

One of the best things we can do for our future selves is to build up resilience. There are ways to cultivate it without needing to go through difficult times—ways that help you prepare for the next battle and be victorious a lot quicker than before.

HOW GRATITUDE HELPS US BOUNCE BACK FROM ADVERSITY

It can be very trying to still remain grateful in the face of adversity. However, it's probably the most important time to be grateful. Practicing gratitude when nothing seems to be going right helps us to keep our focus on what matters and what makes life worth living. By disregarding what we have to be grateful for, we might find ourselves in a situation where nothing seems to be worth it. And that is a very dangerous place to be.

If you've been there before, or you are there now, don't worry. Most of us have been there, and it's nothing to be ashamed of. What's important is to acknowledge what is happening and start putting things into place that can help you get into a better mindset. Into a gratitude mindset.

When we practice gratitude during difficult times, it energizes us. It lifts our spirits enough to help us push through. In fact, it could even help us make it look easy. When we focus on the bad and everything that is going wrong, we give that center stage, and it will start overflowing into all the other aspects of our lives. The same is true when focusing on the good. We want the good, the gratitude, to flow into every aspect of our lives.

It may be challenging to feel grateful during these times because we can't control how we feel. So, don't expect yourself to just *feel* grateful when the storm is brewing. The good news is that you can *be* grateful for everything else and shift your perspective when things get difficult. It's not an easy task to do, but it's definitely worth it.

Let's look at some activities that can help us work through this.

Activity Twenty-Nine: Adversity Gratitude Journaling

We know we will face adversity, so let's prepare for it. For this activity, we will focus on some of the challenging times that you had to go through and then find something that you can be grateful for in the midst of that.

Get a journal, book, or even a blank Word document. Write down some of the adversities you've had to face, whether recent or not. Try to record it in as much detail as possible. Once done, look for things that you can be grateful for instead, whether directly related to the event or not. For example, you may be grateful for the opportunity to learn from your mistakes, or you may be grateful that you had people around you to support you during that time.

By doing this, we are training our minds to look at the difficult times from another perspective where we are grateful instead of stressed out.

Activity Thirty: Reflecting on Past Experiences

This activity flows directly from the previous. This is where we acknowledge what we learned from these adversities.

Once you have taken time to reflect on your adversities noted in Activity Twenty-Nine, this should come quite easily. Try to identify at least one skill you gained or one thing you learned from each of these situations.

Identifying what we got out of the situation will help us to accept adversity in our lives because we acknowledge that we can get something valuable from it.

DEVELOP COPING SKILLS AND RESILIENCE

Everyone is always talking about resilience and how they have built up resilience. I know I always mentioned it earlier in this chapter, but what is resilience actually and what does someone who is resilient look like?

Resilience is the ability to quickly recover or bounce back after challenging times. Someone who is resilient finds it easier to deal with and recover from a challenging situation. They don't shut down and allow the situation to overwhelm them.

By regularly practicing gratitude, we can rewire our brains to be more resilient. Being grateful has a ripple effect on every aspect of our lives, and we become more fulfilled, more positive, and more connected to our situations. We remain focused on the now and what we have instead of what is going wrong or what we're lacking.

There are two main ways gratitude helps us to develop coping skills and resilience. Firstly, by focusing on the positive, we are more creative, and it's easier for us to find solutions to our problems. The second way gratitude helps is that it encourages us to look for support from others.

Here are some fun ways to practice gratitude while building resilience and better coping skills.

Activity Thirty-One: Gratitude Conversations

Learning from others is always an excellent way to build up our own toolbox. There will always be someone with more resilience than us that we can learn from.

Find someone that you admire because of their resilience and ability to cope under pressure. Arrange to have a coffee or a chat with them and ask them about the gratitude practices that they use and how these have helped them to become more resilient.

Hearing first-hand from other people about their experiences and what works for them is a lot different than just reading about it. It's a whole different experience. Remember that what works for one person might not work for the next. Although it's important to learn from others, don't use it as a hard-and-fast rule and then think you are doing something wrong if it yields no results. You need to find methods that work for you.

Activity Thirty-Two: Gratitude Trips

Taking a gratitude trip involves going somewhere that we enjoy going to or where we can experience gratitude at another level.

Take a gratitude trip to visit a place that you are grateful for, whether due to the beauty or the experiences you've had there. It can even be a place where you've faced great difficulty in the past but that has shaped you into the amazing person you are now. Take some time to just absorb everything you can from the experience.

Sometimes, we need a little more help to be grateful for something. Visiting places that we really appreciate and enjoy going to is a great way to get our mindset right and kickstart the right attitude.

Activity Thirty-Three: Gratitude Pause

We all need to take a pause every now and then, especially on busy days. A gratitude pause is when we take some time out from the day and just appreciate the current moment.

If you are having a particularly busy day, take a few minutes for a gratitude pause. Take a few deep breaths to help get you in a calm state if you feel like it's necessary, and then express some things that you can be grateful for in that moment.

It doesn't matter whether you have one thing or ten things. Expressing gratitude in that moment will help to refocus and make you feel better. I especially like to take a gratitude pause when I'm feeling overwhelmed. It helps to calm and clear my mind to deal with the day better.

CULTIVATING GRATITUDE DURING DIFFICULT TIMES

In addition to what we've already covered, here are some ways to cultivate gratitude when things get tough:

- **Spread it on Social Media:** We all love social media. We're all connected. With all the bad news that's always doing the rounds, why not spread some good news? Share something positive and uplifting on social media. It doesn't have to be something personal. You can even share an article on gratitude or a Webinar that someone is hosting.
- **Stay away from the negatives:** If someone is always sharing negative energy, nothing forces you to be part of it. Try to stay away from the Negative Nancys who never have anything positive to add. We start acting like those around us, so if we are continually surrounded by

someone who is negative, then it will start to rub off on us.

- **Be surrounded by the greats:** On that note, make sure that you surround yourself with those who are overachievers. The ones that overflow with gratitude and confidence. You can see them from a mile away. Their greatness will rub off on you.

- **Celebrate the small things:** Make a big deal of the small wins. Didn't express a negative thought the whole day? Score! Celebrate it! Did you remember to write in your gratitude journal this morning? Celebrate! However small it may seem, celebrating the small things will help us remain focused on what's important.

- **Compliment someone:** Okay, this is more for the other person, but you will also feel good after you see what effect it has on the other person. All it takes to make someone's day better is a heartfelt compliment. When you see something beautiful in someone, speak it. If a stranger is wearing a cool shirt, tell them you like their shirt and that they have a good fashion sense. Whatever it is, just tell them!

CHAPTER 5 SUMMARY

- Another amazing benefit of gratitude is that it helps us to be more resilient and bounce back from adversity.
- Developing coping skills and resilience is a natural byproduct of practicing gratitude.

- There are many ways to express gratitude during difficult times, including sharing positivity on social media, steering clear of negative people, surrounding yourself with positive people, celebrating small wins, and giving someone else a compliment.

While gratitude can definitely help us to bounce back from adversity and foster resilience, it has even more benefits. Next, we will discuss the connection between gratitude and happiness and how we can appreciate the daily joys of life.

FINDING JOY IN EVERYDAY LIFE

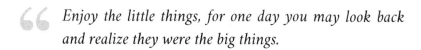

Enjoy the little things, for one day you may look back and realize they were the big things.

— ROBERT BRAULT

W ouldn't it be nice if every day were different? If we had something to look forward to and do something exciting every day of our lives, like having a weekend all of the time. Although some people can afford to live a life like that, most of us are stuck in the normal day-to-day life where most of our days are the same. We do the same things and look forward to the weekend when things might be a little different. We live for those moments when things are more exciting. But every day is a gift. If we just focus our attention on the good, we can appreciate every single day.

Being able to have dinner with the family might be something you don't particularly enjoy. "But, Mom, I want to eat in my room!" We've all been there. The thing is, one day, when you live alone, you will miss being able to sit around the table and have dinner with the family. Or have someone that annoys you while you are watching television. These moments should be treasured.

But how do we do that? How can we find joy in daily, mundane tasks?

HOW GRATITUDE ENHANCES POSITIVE EMOTIONS AND SATISFACTION

It should come as no surprise that practicing gratitude regularly enhances positive emotions and improves life satisfaction. We've briefly touched on this in earlier chapters.

By expressing gratitude for what we have, we train our minds to focus on the positives, which improves our outlook on life. If we focus on what we're lacking, which is the opposite of gratitude, that's all we will ever see.

Although there have been quite a few studies done to prove this, I want you to conduct a little experiment yourself. Activity Thirty-Four involves tracking your mood before and after you express gratitude for something. Let's see whether there is a difference, shall we?

Activity Thirty-Four: Gratitude Mood Tracker

A mood tracker is something you use to track your mood during the week or even the day. It helps us to pick up any trends, like a dip in our mood during a certain time of the day or week.

Create a mood tracker where you can note down your mood first thing in the morning. Note it again before you practice gratitude and again immediately after. It's important to name the emotion you are feeling as accurately as possible. If you are not too familiar with the different emotions, there are many resources online that can help.

How you choose to track your mood is also important. It should be something that you enjoy, and that's quite easy to do. Many people choose a bullet journal to create their own, but you also get gratitude journals that have a mood tracker already built in. You can also find some apps for your mobile phone that can do the job just as well.

Make sure that you go back to review and reflect on your different moods. You can do it at the end of the day or week or even at the end of the month.

A mood tracker has many benefits. It helps us to regulate our emotions much better, empowers us to name the emotion we are experiencing, and helps us to identify how our emotions change when we change our state of mind by practicing gratitude.

Activity Thirty-Five: Personal Achievements

Personal achievements can be a range of different things and will be different for each person. What I think is an amazing achievement might not be something you consider great.

For this activity, make a list of all the personal achievements that you are proud of and grateful for. Try to identify any resources or people that helped you achieve those and see whether there is any sort of trend. Express gratitude for anything or anyone that helped you or supported you.

Sometimes, we need to take stock of what we already have done to motivate us to do even greater things. Reflecting on some of the things we've achieved is an amazing way to remain humble, grateful for what we have, and motivated to keep on going.

FINDING AND APPRECIATING JOY IN DAILY EXPERIENCES

We've already established that gratitude can lead to increased fulfillment, positivity, and overall happiness. Here are some practical guidelines to help you find joy wherever you go. While practicing these, make sure to incorporate gratitude into the moment.

- **Talk to people:** Whether it's family, friends, or even a stranger you meet on your commute, talking to other people and connecting with them helps us to feel happier. We find more fulfillment in life when we can relate to others. Just a lovely conversation with another person will instantly improve the day.

- **Add a splash of color:** You'd be surprised what some color can do. Introduce bright colors to your room or even the home. It doesn't have to be everywhere, but a splash of color can go a long way. It has a big impact on our emotions, and the right colors can make us feel a lot more calm, peaceful and happy.

- **Make a joy list:** Think about everything that makes you joyful and make a list of it. Just like a gratitude list, a list of things that bring you joy is the perfect thing to turn to when the day seems tough.

- **Get a house plant:** That might sound silly, but it's been scientifically proven that just seeing, feeling, and smelling house plants can reduce stress and make people happier (Lee et al., 2015).

- **Exercise:** You thought we wouldn't cover it in this book. Exercise is very good for you and every aspect of your health. Taking some time out of your day, even if it's just 10 minutes, will make a difference. When we exercise, we release feel-good hormones that make us happy. It doesn't have to be running or going to the gym. Find an exercise you enjoy, like swimming, yoga, or even dancing.

- **Spend more time outside:** Fresh air, the sun, and chirping birds have a way of making us feel happier. My mom once told me that whenever I feel a little meh, I should eat a banana while sitting outside in the sun, and I promise you it has made me feel better every single time. Spending time outside will boost your mood and make you appreciate nature more.

- **Be on the lookout for new experiences:** I know the unknown can sometimes be scary, but it's always a good idea to try something new. Look for new markets that you can visit, new skills to cultivate, or even new places to grab a bite to eat.

Let's see how we can practically incorporate this into our daily lives.

Activity Thirty-Six: Joyful Moments Reflection

We've seen that moments of joy can exist in our daily lives. It's important to recognize these moments and appreciate them when we encounter them.

Take a moment to reflect on your day and note down any possible moments of joy during the day. Identify any aspects that contributed to them and how you felt when it was happening. Express gratitude for these moments of joy that you were able to experience today.

We get so caught up in daily life that we sometimes miss these moments of joy. By paying special attention to them, we make ourselves more sensitive to what they might look like on an otherwise mundane day and can focus on them to bring some light to our lives.

Activity Thirty-Seven: Gratitude for Routine

We have a routine because it works. It might not always be fun to do, and sometimes it can start feeling a little repetitive, but showing gratitude for something that works might help us look at it differently.

Think about all the routines you have on any given day. Reflect on the reason for those routines and whether things would run as smoothly if things were just left up to chance instead of having a routine. Identify those routines that, although mundane, make a big difference in terms of bringing you peace of mind and joy when things work out.

We can easily get caught up in the motions of the day. When we get too used to a routine, it might start feeling mundane, and we are more likely to fall into a negative mindset because of it. Although some people suggest that you should mix it up, some routines are there to ensure order and peace of mind. Without it, things could easily turn into chaos! Appreciating these routines can give us a new sense of understanding and appreciation for the mundane.

Activity Thirty-Eight: Gratitude Photography

Not everyone is a photographer, and that's fine. That doesn't mean we can't all benefit from the joys that taking photos may bring. Gratitude photography is all about taking marvelous photos and appreciating what has now been captured in a frame.

If you are into photography and have a fancy camera, I would suggest you use that. But if you don't, please don't feel like you need to buy one to get the full experience. Photographs on your phone will absolutely do the exact same thing! I have even seen photographs from some of the new smartphones that look better than photographs taken with a digital camera.

Take some time to look around your environment for anything that catches your eye. We sometimes miss the most amazing things because we don't really pay attention, like a spider spinning a new web. Capture any moments that bring you joy and express gratitude for those photographs. You can even print them out and add them to your gratitude board.

CHAPTER 6 SUMMARY

- Life doesn't always have to be boring just because the bulk of our days are the same.
- There are ways that we can find joy and feel more fulfilled. This includes:

  ○ Having conversations with people, adding color to our lives, making a list of things that bring us joy, getting a house plant (or ten), exercising, spending some time outdoors, and looking for new things to do.

There is a strong link between gratitude and happiness, and gratitude can enhance life satisfaction. In Chapter 7, we will dive a little deeper into how gratitude enhances our physical health.

GRATITUDE AND PHYSICAL WELL-BEING

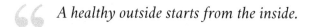 *A healthy outside starts from the inside.*

— ROBERT URICH

I love my sleep. I can't imagine having to deal with insomnia, but I also know that there are quite a few people who do. In fact, recent statistics from Hull (2022) confirm that the most common sleep disorder in the USA is insomnia and up to 30% of adults in the USA experience insomnia.

I have dealt with quite a few insomniacs in my line of work. Some of them had it so bad that they were completely dependent on sleeping tablets just to get some sleep at night, not even a good night's rest. Whenever I've suggested that they practice more mindfulness and gratitude to improve sleep, I've always received skepticism. During those encounters, I tried to start small to get them into it, and eventually, they embraced it fully.

Needless to say, they were pleasantly surprised that their sleeping habits improved drastically after only a few activities of gratitude.

I'm sure they're not the only ones who are skeptical when it comes to gratitude and physical well-being. We always link gratitude to emotional and mental well-being, but what about physical well-being? Is there a possibility that gratitude can help us sleep better and cure some physical aches that we might experience?

The doctor definitely won't write you a prescription for gratitude when you need it, but there have been a few studies (and I have had first-hand experience!) where participants showed improved physical health as a result of practicing gratitude.

CONNECTION BETWEEN GRATITUDE AND PHYSICAL HEALTH

There have been quite a few debates on this topic. Although some studies do seem to support that gratitude improves physical health, others argue that it might just be that unhealthy people have less to be grateful for.

Seems like a fair observation, and I would agree that we need to explore this a little more to get a final answer.

A study done by Simon-Thomas (2012) challenged participants to practice gratitude through an online journal for two weeks, and at the end, the participants reported that they had better skin, physical ailments, and less congestion after the study than before.

There are some studies where the effects of gratitude seemed to have made no difference. However, these studies were of short duration, which might indicate that gratitude needs to be practiced for an extended period of time to improve physical health.

This is the perfect opportunity to express gratitude for our health.

Activity Thirty-Nine: Gratitude for Health

We are all guilty of taking our physical health for granted, but getting up in the morning and being able to see, hear, and speak are all blessings we should be grateful for.

Take some time today to write down or even mentally note down all the things related to your physical health that you are grateful for. Start from the top and work your way down. I already gave you three ideas above. Now, you just need to fill in the rest.

Expressing gratitude for our physical health will make us feel happier and healthier. The more we practice gratitude for our physical health, the healthier we will become. It really is a win-win situation.

Activity Forty: Gratitude Yoga

Yoga involves putting your body in nearly impossible positions and keeping it in that position for an extended period of time. That's what we've been taught to believe. However, there are yoga poses that are doable for normal people like you and me.

So, if you are not super flexible and you've tried and failed at yoga before, don't skip this activity. We're in this together.

While doing the yoga poses, express gratitude for your body and physical health. Here is how you can incorporate gratitude into yoga:

- Before you start, set an intention of gratitude.
- Remember to breathe throughout, and with every breath, count your blessings. As you breathe in, express gratitude for something and allow it to flow into the rest of your body as you breathe out.
- If it gets challenging, smile about it. We tend to tighten our face during yoga (and life) when things get difficult. Make a point to smile instead.

Here are a few beginner poses that you might want to research and try:

- standing forward fold
- seated forward fold
- camel pose
- corpse pose
- the mountain pose with raised hands
- child's pose (a personal favorite)
- knees-to-chest

Know your limits and only stretch as far as you can. Yoga has many benefits. It helps us to calm our mind; it's a type of exercise, gets us to be more flexible, and helps with gratitude. Really an all-in-one!

GRATITUDE AND IMPROVED SLEEP

Have you ever been too excited or too anxious to sleep? Physiologically, excitement and anxiety are the same. We experience the same symptoms, but the emotions are just different. The emotions we experience are what tell our brain whether we are excited or anxious. So, it's normal for both anxiety and excitement to result in difficulty sleeping.

Gratitude can help our minds to calm down. If there is one thing you should have picked up by now during these gratitude activities, it is that gratitude helps to create a calm atmosphere and serenity. Practicing gratitude before bed is the ideal way to help bring order to your thoughts and allow sleep to come.

In addition to practicing gratitude, here are some other things to work into your bedtime routine to help you fall asleep:

- Make sure that your bedroom is only used for sleeping. When we do other things there, like doing our homework or watching television, our brains are not sure what it's supposed to do when we're in our bedrooms. By only sleeping there, our brain immediately knows that when we go there at night, it's to fall asleep.
- Have a full-on routine so that your brain and body know what is next. A bedtime routine is not just for

babies. Our brains like structure and knowing what to expect next.

- Make sure that you exercise well before bed. Exercising too close to bed can cause difficulty falling asleep.
- Avoid any sugary and caffeinated food and drink two to three hours before bedtime.

Let's jump into the activity to apply the above knowledge.

Activity Forty-One: Gratitude Before Sleep

It's clear from the above section that gratitude before bed can improve sleep. So, today, we are going to express gratitude before we sleep in an attempt to get an even better night's rest.

As you prepare for bed, stay away from all electronic devices for at least an hour. This has nothing to do with gratitude but is part of good sleep hygiene. It's difficult for our brains to move over to sleep mode if we keep stimulating it. Keep your gratitude journal next to your bed. Just before you call it a night, make a list of a few things that you are grateful for. When you wake up in the morning, reflect on how you slept and write it down. Keep track of your sleeping habits and see how it improves over time.

By expressing gratitude just before bed, we calm our minds and help good hormones to be released. This should improve sleep from the very first night, even if only slightly. The longer you practice it, the more benefits you will reap.

I challenged one of the teens I work with to do this recently, and although she didn't think much of it, I have seen a clear difference in her overall attitude and the way she carries herself. She has admitted to being more joyful and seeing the good in situations instead of always getting worked up about everything. Her outlook on life has changed, and she went from always feeling like she needs to fight back to someone who turns the other cheek and tries to find solutions to problems she encounters. It has also had an impact on her sleep—about a week after she started, she reported higher energy levels and that she wasn't feeling as tired during the day anymore. That is a clear indication of improved sleep quality.

GRATITUDE PROMOTES BETTER CARDIOVASCULAR HEALTH AND IMMUNE FUNCTION

Although the exact science has not been revealed yet, Huffman et al. (2015) conducted a study on patients who recently had an acute coronary event. The study revealed that those who practiced gratitude after the event had a quicker recovery rate and a healthier heart than those who didn't.

Another study done by Mills et al. (2015) yielded similar results, confirming that heart failure patients who were more grateful for what they had in life and practiced gratitude more often were much healthier than those who didn't.

There are many other studies where the link between gratitude and immune function, as well as cardiovascular health, is measured, and gratitude is slowly becoming one of the top contributors to better heart and immune function. Is there anything gratitude can't do?

With this knowledge, let's express gratitude for our hearts and immune function.

Activity Forty-Two: Gratitude for a Beating Heart

How much thought do we give to our heart beating? None at all. It just does it without being asked and without us needing to actively do anything for it to beat. Let's take some time to acknowledge the hard work it does and appreciate that it's keeping us alive.

For this activity, make sure that you are wearing comfortable clothes. Sit down on the floor in a comfortable position and take three deep breaths. Now, place either two of your fingers on your wrist or neck or even place a hand over your heart. Make sure that you can feel your heartbeat. Take your time to find it. Sometimes it's harder than other times.

When you can feel it, close your eyes and just stay in the moment, appreciating how fast or slow it's beating. Make a mental note of how fast or slow it's beating, as well as the emotion you are feeling in that moment. Stay in this moment for as long as you need to.

This is a great activity to shine the spotlight on our hearts and the amazing work it's doing. You will feel better, more relaxed, and (dare I say it) healthier.

Activity Forty-Three: Gratitude for Immunity

There is something else that keeps us healthy, and that's our immune system. We can't forget to also acknowledge our immune system and appreciate the hard work it does to protect us from diseases.

Following the same steer as in Activity Forty-Two, sit up straight and take three deep breaths. Instead of feeling for your heartbeat, you can just take another few deep breaths and, with every breath, express gratitude for your immune system. Imagine that the air you are breathing in is replaced with gratitude, and this flows through your entire body to thank your immune system. Take your time with this exercise.

Just like with our hearts, it's important to appreciate the unsung heroes of our body for working tirelessly to keep us going. It will improve our gratitude mindset and change our focus.

CHAPTER 7 SUMMARY

- There are many studies that support the fact that gratitude can have a positive effect on:

  - our physical health in terms of aches and pains.
  - our sleeping patterns.
  - our cardiovascular health.
  - our immune function.

Gratitude is useful for everything. If there was ever a doubt in your mind, I hope this book has convinced you. In the next chapter, we will cover some practical exercises for incorporating gratitude into our daily routines and how to establish lasting habits.

BEING GRATEFUL IS A DAILY PRACTICE

> *Gratitude can transform common days into thanksgiving, turn routine jobs into joy, and change ordinary opportunities into blessings.*
>
> — WILLIAM ARTHUR WARD

I hear you. All of this is great, but these have all been guided activities, so how does this translate to daily living once the book is finished and some time has passed? Because let's be honest, while information is fresh, it's easier to apply it. But it soon becomes a distant memory, and then we forget to apply anything we learned.

It's important to take these aspects and incorporate them into our daily routines. It should come as naturally as breathing—we shouldn't even have to think about it.

It can be hard to do that without proper guidelines, which is why I have dedicated Chapter 8 to provide you with some practical guidelines on how you can easily incorporate practicing gratitude into your daily life.

INCORPORATING GRATITUDE INTO DAILY ROUTINES

A daily routine is something we perform every day. Wouldn't it be amazing if we could add gratitude as part of our routine? Here are some ways you can do it. Remember, you don't have to apply all of them. Find what works for you and stick to it.

- **Commit to journaling:** We've done some exercises when it comes to journaling. Find the one you like most, and make a point of it to do it every single day. When the journal is full, buy another one. Very few things in life are quite as fulfilling as paging through a full gratitude journal and reminiscing.
- **Before you eat:** It's probably one of the easiest ways to incorporate gratitude. Every time before a meal, just mention one thing that you are thankful for today and why. You can do this silently, or, if the whole family dines together, ask each person to share something. By involving the whole family, someone is bound to remember this fun little activity before everyone starts eating.
- **Side-step the gossip:** Whenever someone starts talking about someone else behind their back, excuse yourself from the conversation. We shouldn't get involved in

those kinds of conversations at all. It creates animosity, which completely overshadows gratitude.

- **Set reminders:** It's widely accepted to set reminders for anything else, like waking up, taking medication, or even for a show we want to watch. Why not set one to remember to practice gratitude? It's one of the best ways to keep yourself accountable. But don't just dismiss the alarm and not do it. It defeats the purpose of setting one.

- **Visual reminders:** We are so fortunate to live in a world where technology has made everything easier for us. By setting our phone's background to something or someone we are grateful for (such as a family picture), we can be reminded to be grateful every time we look at our wallpaper. Change them up to keep the exercise fresh and evolving. This also makes it easier to be grateful first thing in the morning. As soon as I open my eyes, I check my phone for any messages or emails that may have come through during the night. By being reminded first thing in the morning to be grateful, we set ourselves up to have a much better day.

- **Take a walk:** If it's possible, swap your morning ride for a brisk walk to school and take time to appreciate your surroundings. You can take a gratitude walk from Activity Two every morning!

- **Turn up the motivation:** When you turn on the television or your computer to watch YouTube or play games, make a point of it to first watch a motivational video that will encourage gratitude.

- **Smile!** I think we all look at ourselves in any mirror or window that we walk past. As soon as you see yourself, let that serve as a reminder to smile. Smiling immediately boosts your mood and can make others feel more at ease around you, too.

- **Spend time with those you value:** When we spend time with the people we care most about, gratitude comes easy. We get reminded of how much they elevate our lives, and that feeling of appreciation and happiness lingers long after the meeting is over.

- **Steer clear of the negative:** It's all around us, I know. But don't entertain it. Make a conscious effort to focus on the good whenever you hear of anything bad happening in the world.

- **Offer up your free time:** Not all of it, but commit to a non-profit organization that you can help out at least once a month. I like to do it on the last Saturday of every month.

- **Just be nice:** Show patience and kindness to everyone you meet. It doesn't cost you anything to just be nice. Express gratitude instead of losing your patience. The only person affected by your behavior and attitude is you. Don't allow anything or anyone else to spoil your day.

If the above isn't enough, let's look at some activities that we can do.

Activity Forty-Four: Gratitude Alarm

This is a fun activity for the day. We are going to set some alarms to remind us to express gratitude for something in that moment.

Don't choose specific times, but set up random alarms throughout the day. About ten should do it. As soon as one of them goes off, pause with whatever you are busy with and think of something that you are grateful for. It doesn't have to be something related to what you are doing but try to mention something different every time.

This activity forces us to stop and smell the flowers. We get so busy with our daily lives that it's easy to forget. You don't have to do this every single day, but it's nice every now and then. Maybe try doing it once a month.

Activity Forty-Five: Gratitude During Chores

I don't think I know anyone who enjoys chores. There might be one or two things that we don't mind doing, but definitely not like. A great spin to put on it is to express gratitude while doing chores like washing the dishes, cleaning our rooms, and so on.

Next time you need to do some chores, bring gratitude into it. If you are cleaning your room, express gratitude for every item you need to pack away. For example, if you are throwing dirty clothes in the washing, express gratitude for the clothes you have. Think about and be grateful for the person who does the washing. When making your bed, express how grateful you are to have a bed and a blanket that keeps you warm. Be thankful for the pillow you have to rest your head on. You get where I'm going.

Incorporating gratitude into doing chores is an excellent way to express gratitude daily. By doing this, we're more aware of what we have and that we have the honor to perform these chores. Having to make your bed means that you have a bed to sleep on. Having dishes to wash means there was something to eat. We can always find something to be grateful for.

DISCUSSING THE IMPORTANCE OF CONSISTENCY AND REGULAR PRACTICE

To be good at anything, you have to be consistent in your practice. If you are not, it's very unlikely that you will achieve anything great. A fulfilled life doesn't just fall from the sky—we have to put effort in to achieve it and remain consistent to keep it going.

Those who are unsuccessful in their endeavors have one thing in common: they lack consistency and self-discipline. To succeed, you need to be consistent.

Consistency is about repeating the same action to reach a goal. When you commit to do something, you follow through and don't give up halfway. Consistency leads to success, and success leads to a more fulfilled life.

There are many reasons why some of us struggle with consistency. These may include feeling unfocused, not having a clear goal in mind, being impatient, or wanting instant gratification. Practicing gratitude will not always lead to instant gratification. Some of the benefits develop over time, so you need to be consistent.

Here's why consistency is important:

- **Building trust:** There are certain things that I know I will never do, and then there are others that I can trust myself to do. Being consistent helps to build and stretch that trust. It also helps others to trust you more.
- **Cultivating self-discipline and self-control:** It's easier to fall back on what we're used to than to create new habits. When we are consistent, we teach ourselves self-discipline by keeping ourselves accountable.
- **Reaching goals:** To reach goals, we need to be consistent. The more consistent we are, the faster we can reach our goals. If we backslide a bit, we can always get back on track, but it will take longer to get where we want to be.
- **It's contagious:** People are drawn to those who are consistent because they know that results will follow. We naturally gravitate toward those who have skills that we admire and would like to cultivate.

If we don't consistently and mindfully practice gratitude, all of the work we've put in so far will be for nothing. Practicing gratitude has life-long benefits, and in order to experience those, we need to be consistent. When we move our focus away from gratitude, the negativity can easily absorb us, and we'll be back at square one.

ESTABLISHING GRATITUDE HABITS FOR A LASTING CHANGE

What is the best way to remain consistent with something? You make it a habit! But to make it a habit, you also need to be consistent. The two are dependent on each other. For this reason, developing habits can be difficult. Replacing bad habits with ones that are better for us is even harder.

To create new habits, we need to understand the habit loop, which is, luckily, quite easy to understand. There are three parts to the habit loop: the cue, the action or routine, and the reward. The reward needs to be worth it. Otherwise, it will never become a habit. Let's use a bad habit, such as eating take-out, as an example. There's nothing wrong with having takeout every now and then, but when it becomes a habit, it's a problem.

The cue for takeout might be hunger, you just got money, or even the fact that it's Friday. The cue is always the same. The action or routine is to buy takeout. The reward is that it tastes good. However, the long-term effect of regular takeout is not that rewarding. That's the thing about a habit. It's about what the action or routine can deliver right now. This is why so many people smoke even though they know it's bad for their health. They feel like it helps them calm down or something to that effect.

The more we perform the same thing in response to the same cue, the stronger the connections for that specific action become in our brain. To take it back a bit, our brains are made up of neurons that send signals to the rest of our body. Actions that we perform most have a stronger neural pathway, that is, a stronger connection from the one part of the brain where the cue is received to the other part of the brain where the action is performed. Eventually, we don't even have to think about the action we are performing. Our body already knows exactly what to do in response to the cue.

Think about brushing your teeth. When you were small, you might have had a little rhyme to remember exactly where to brush, how to brush, and for how long. When you brush your teeth now, it has become such an automatic action that you don't really need to think about it anymore. This is why it can be very difficult to change old habits because you need to make a conscious effort to change the way you normally react to the same cue.

Creating a gratitude habit would, therefore, be ideal. Whenever the cue comes up, we will automatically express gratitude. Be careful not to fall into the trap of practicing gratitude without being mindful. Make sure that whenever you express gratitude, you are sincere and specific about it. Being thankful for the same things every day can become easy to practice, but it won't have the same effect because you are not doing it mindfully or purposefully. Don't let it become just another tick-box exercise.

The best way to learn is to put it into practice. Let's go!

Activity Forty-Six: Gratitude Routine

We are creatures of habit. We like to have a routine and stick to it, for the most part. Just like we have to follow our nighttime routine every day, we can also create a gratitude routine. Establishing new routines is like establishing a habit. Eventually, our routines become habits.

Make a list of what you want to include in your gratitude routine, and decide when in the day you want to do it. Make sure that you slot it in where it's convenient so that you don't have to ever skip it simply because there's no time. Whether it's early in the morning, late at night, or somewhere in between, it needs to fit into your current daily routine. We all have one.

Add any of the gratitude activities to the list that we've been going through in this book. Anything that really stuck with you and you really enjoyed. The routine doesn't have to be hours long. A daily 10-minute routine is more than enough.

Building a gratitude routine into our daily routine makes it easier to practice gratitude and remain consistent.

Activity Forty-Seven: Habit Stacking

Habit stacking is the simple practice of performing something that you would like to make a habit, together with an already established habit. An example would be doing squats while brushing your teeth. You have to brush your teeth twice a day. You only need one hand to do it, so you might as well do something with your legs while you have the time.

For this activity, we want to try the habit stacking gratitude with something that we habitually do. It may be different for everyone, so really think about the habit that you want to connect it to. Here are some examples:

- While you are eating (mindful eating).
- While doing chores (like we discussed in Activity Forty-Five).
- When we get ready for the day. Most of the time, you'll be looking in the mirror, so that's the perfect time to do some gratitude mirror exercises.
- While taking a bath or a shower.

Make sure that you can commit to practicing gratitude together with these habits and always do it. You might forget the first few times, so leave a note for yourself to remember. If you want to do it while getting ready, you can leave a note on the mirror. Put it somewhere where you know you will look while you are performing the habit.

This is one of the easiest ways to cultivate new habits because we connect it to a habit we've already perfected.

Activity Forty-Eight: Reward System

There's nothing better than getting rewarded for something. That's why it's also an aspect of creating new habits. As humans, we like being rewarded for what we've done. Creating a reward system is a great way to motivate ourselves to do something. Try to set up a reward system for when you've consistently practiced gratitude for a period of time.

The first thing you need to do is think about all the things that will motivate you to do something. What rewards can you offer yourself that will get you to remain consistent? Have small rewards and bigger ones, but make sure that they all mean something to you.

Next, you want to set up some kind of reward chart. Using a monthly calendar of some sort, or even creating your own, can work. Decide how often you think you will need to be rewarded. This will be different from person to person. Some people can work toward a goal for a month with no reward and remain consistent, while others need daily rewards to stay motivated. Find out what your limit is and try to stretch it every time. For example, if you need daily rewards in the beginning, start stretching it to every two days and then once a week. I think once a week is a good start, but choose something that you know you will keep to.

Now, choose rewards for every milestone. If you need daily rewards, try to keep them small in the beginning, like getting an ice cream, and increase the reward as time goes on. Maybe have a big reward at the end of the month if you've been consistent and practiced gratitude every day for the whole month.

If you skip a day, you start all over again. This will help you to remain consistent. Once you've got it under the knee and gratitude becomes a habit, you can stretch the rewards even more or remove them completely. It's really up to you.

By rewarding ourselves for doing good, we're motivating our brains to perform the task we want it to. It's an effective way to get on track.

CHAPTER 8 SUMMARY

- Making gratitude a daily practice can be done by incorporating it into some of the daily routines we have. Some examples include journaling, expressing gratitude before a meal, avoiding gossip, setting reminders, having visual reminders, taking a walk instead of opting for a ride, watching motivational videos, smiling, spending time with the ones we value most, avoiding negative propaganda, offering up our time to charitable organizations, and being a nice person overall.
- Being consistent is the key to success. If we don't consistently practice gratitude, it's something that will easily become forgotten.
- The best way to remain consistent is to create a habit out of it. There are excellent ways to make gratitude a habit, including creating a gratitude routine, habit stacking, and having a reward system.

It's easy to incorporate gratitude into our daily routines if we know where to fit it in and how to trick our brains into creating a habit out of it. In the last chapter, I have included a guide to 31 days of gratitude.

31 DAYS OF GRATITUDE

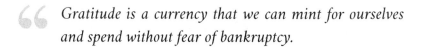 *Gratitude is a currency that we can mint for ourselves and spend without fear of bankruptcy.*

— FRED DE WITT VAN AMBURGH

I will leave you with a final challenge, which is 31-days of gratitude. You should take 31 days to complete this challenge. It's important to only do one a day to reap the full benefit of these activities.

Some of these activities may be similar to the ones we did in the earlier chapters. These were just to lay the foundation and help you to foster a habit of practicing gratitude. Even if you did these as part of the chapter activities, don't skip them here! You don't have to do them in this exact order, but it might be easier to keep track of if you do.

If you want to put a little spin on it, write down each day on a piece of paper and add them all to a jar or box. Draw one every day and complete the task. If you opt for this option, don't cheat. If you draw an activity, you have to do it.

Take 5 to 10 minutes each day to complete these activities. If you need to, set a daily alarm to remind yourself to complete the challenge. After each activity or challenge, say "thank you" three times to close it off.

Day 1: Write down three things that you are grateful for today with a reason why. Adding the reason makes us think harder about our answer and not just write down the first thing that we can think of.

Day 2: Write a letter or a thank you note to the person who has impacted your life in the biggest and best way. You can also write a message on social media if you prefer, but make sure that it's a heartfelt note.

Day 3: Reflect on a challenging situation you had to deal with recently and find things that you can be grateful for. Write down what you learned from it and express gratitude for the opportunity.

Day 4: Write down five things that give you joy in your life right now and take some time to appreciate them. If you have more than five, that's great!

Day 5: Take a walk outside or spend a few minutes in nature and appreciate the beauty. Reflect on things that you appreciate from nature. If you can't find anything, look for any insects and observe them for a few minutes. You'd be amazed at what they do!

Day 6: We're back with mindful eating. Practice it today with all the meals you have and just become appreciative of the food and the process it went through to get to a point where you can eat it. Consider the people who worked to get the food, take it to the supermarket, and the person who bought it and made a meal out of it.

Day 7: Write a gratitude letter to yourself where you appreciate your strengths and everything that you've accomplished so far. You can even add some areas of improvement and express gratitude for the ability and/or opportunity to improve yourself.

Day 8: Appreciate your body today and do some mindfulness exercises or gentle stretching. Don't push yourself too far, and know your limits.

Day 9: Express gratitude for something specific every hour of the day. Be mindful and try to mention something different every time. Use alarms to remind yourself, if needed.

Day 10: Take some time to reflect on some of your best birthdays. Write down what made them special and take some time to appreciate those things. It might be people, places, the effort that went into it, or even the thoughtful gifts you received.

Day 11: Today is a meditation and gratitude breathing day. Practice some deep breathing and focus on gratitude and positivity throughout.

Day 12: Reach out to someone that means a lot to you but you haven't spoken to in a while. Let them know that you are thinking about them and tell them how much you appreciate them.

Day 13: No technology today! This activity is for the whole day. Take a digital detox day and, instead, reflect on everything you are grateful for that has nothing to do with technology. If you feel the urge to reach for your phone or the television remote, practice some gratitude meditation instead or take a gratitude walk.

Day 14: Look at yourself in the mirror and say three things that you appreciate about yourself. These can be physical attributes or characteristics. If you can mention more, don't limit yourself to three.

Day 15: Find a meaningful quote or affirmation that resonates with you and carry it with you the whole day on a piece of paper or even your phone. Repeat it regularly, especially when things get a little tough or busy.

Day 16: Today is a random act of kindness day. Find time to do something for someone else. Note how it makes you feel, then reflect on the impact it had on their day as well.

Day 17: Take a photo of something that you are grateful for and share it with a friend. You can even post it on social media with a gratitude caption and challenge everyone else to do the same.

Day 18: Declutter and organize your personal space. As you do so, appreciate the things you own and the personal space that you have access to.

Day 19: Practice gratitude during meals by saying thank you or silently appreciating the food in front of you. If you are having a meal with family or friends, encourage them to do the same.

Day 20: Make a gratitude list of the people in your life and why you are thankful for them. If you can, let them know that you appreciate them.

Day 21: Spend some time listening to some of your favorite songs. Reflect on the emotions that it stirs inside of you and express gratitude for the power of music and lyrics.

Day 22: Watch a short inspirational video or read an uplifting article. In the end, express gratitude for the positive message that it contains and the motivation it brings.

Day 23: Write down three qualities or skills you possess that you are grateful for and how they have helped you thus far. Think of ways you can improve them even more.

Day 24: Volunteer your time or help someone in need. At the end of the day, reflect on the gratitude that you feel, knowing that you've made a difference in someone else's life.

Day 25: Take a moment to appreciate your hobbies, what interests you, and how they bring you joy. Practice and enjoy them for the day.

Day 26: Make a gratitude list of the opportunities and privileges you have in your life. If there are people who make them possible, express gratitude for them, too.

Day 27: Reflect on recent accomplishments or milestones and express gratitude for the effort it required and the growth that came from it.

Day 28: Practice gratitude for your education by taking a few minutes to appreciate the knowledge and the skills you have obtained and how it has helped you navigate life.

Day 29: Reflect on the past month and write down three ways your gratitude mindset has positively impacted your life.

Day 30: Share your gratitude journey with someone close to you, explaining how it has influenced your perspective and mindset and encouraging them to do the same.

Day 31: Create a gratitude jar or box. Write down one thing each day that you are grateful for over the next 31 days and add it to the jar.

Once you have completed your jar, shake it and take out one note a day. Take a moment to reflect on what is written on the note and be grateful for it. When you have gone through all the notes, rinse and repeat.

You can add more to the jar or box at any point. The aim is to keep practicing gratitude on a continuous basis. The things you are grateful for may even change as you get older, and that's okay. Fostering a culture of gratitude in yourself now will lay the best foundation for your family in the future.

This 31-day challenge is just to get you started. This should definitely not be the end. There are so many other gratitude activities and practices you can do. What I have found works really well and helps me to stay on top of it is involving other people. As soon as I have someone else who does it with me, we keep each other accountable. So, don't forget to have a gratitude buddy. While you are at it, just involve the entire family and make a game out of it. They can definitely all benefit from it!

CONCLUSION

Congratulations on finishing the book. I am so proud of you! It's been amazing to share all I've learned with you, and I really hope you've enjoyed the book. Unfortunately, this is where the book ends, but definitely not your journey. I hope that you will continue with the consistency, and I can't wait to hear about the results you've achieved.

Remember that gratitude is powerful. It can literally influence every aspect of our lives in a positive way! It doesn't come naturally, though, and we need to change the way we think and how we perceive things in order to truly be grateful.

Gratitude has a major impact on our emotional well-being. It's been proven that those who express gratitude more often are happier, and their quality of life is a lot better. Expressing gratitude can make us feel better in an instant, but it also has benefits in the longer term. It can help us to deal better with the symptoms of anxiety and depression and to not feel so over-whelmed.

Gratitude is also amazing when it comes to relationships. The more gratitude there is in a relationship, the healthier the relationship is. We are more inclined to connect with people who show gratitude and have an uplifting spirit because that makes us feel good, too. Plus, it's always nice to be appreciated in a relationship.

In the face of adversity, gratitude is the biggest weapon we can have. It truly helps us to build better resilience by focusing on the good instead of the bad. We bounce back a lot quicker by practicing gratitude.

There is also always something to be grateful for, even in the boring, mundane routines of life. We sometimes miss those small little joys, but gratitude helps us to become mindful of those and make every day a good day.

If that's not enough, there have been multiple studies that show that practicing gratitude is also good for our physical health. It helps to reduce aches and pains, improve our heart health, better sleep, and a stronger immune system. It really seems like there is nothing gratitude can't do.

It took me years to learn all of this, and I am so glad that I was able to share it with you in one book. I have no doubt that you will see a big difference in your life if you apply the principles from this book.

I once worked with someone who didn't have a good life at all. From a very young age, she struggled to make any friends. By the age of thirteen, she was having migraines (something some adults never even experience). She was overweight, didn't enjoy any form of exercise, and, as a result, had quite a low self-esteem. There were so many other things that were going on in her life, and I'm so thankful she found me.

She came to me for help with a few things but never expected to get a solution for all her issues. I'm sure you already know what happened, but let me tell you anyway. We started with small steps toward cultivating gratitude. In the beginning, it was very difficult for her to find much to be grateful for. As time went on and she started making changes in her life, the gratitude started flowing, and now there is no stopping her when she starts.

She has turned her life around a full 180 degrees and never looks back. Today, she is a successful entrepreneur, and everyone loves her. She oozes gratitude, and it's obvious to everyone around her that there is something special about her. The secret really is gratitude! We're busy working through other things now to help her level up even more.

If you also want to level up and learn more, don't forget to take a look at the other books in the Mindset Series. They're called *A Growth Mindset for Teens* and *Money Mindset for Teens & Young Adults*.

If you enjoyed this book, help others to find it by leaving an honest review on Amazon. They're counting on you to show them the right book that can help them, and this book might be exactly what they need to keep going.

Remember, whenever something doesn't feel right in any aspect of your life, try to add a little more gratitude and see whether anything changes. It's the magic medicine that can make (almost) anything better.

Gratitude is a crucial skill that will significantly help you across various areas of life. Apply the lessons you learned from this book and start becoming more grateful today. I can't wait to hear from you.

All my love!

REFERENCES

Allen, S. (2018, March 5). *Is gratitude good for your health?* Greater Good. https://greatergood.berkeley.edu/article/item/ is_gratitude_good_for_your_health

Austin, A. (2018, June 6). *The relationship between gratitude & confidence.* Poised & Professional - Coaching with Alyssa Austin. https://poisedandprofes sional.com/2018/06/why-gratitude-is-the-key-to-becoming-more-confident/

Bostwick, E. (2020, November 10). *Embracing a mindset of gratitude.* Ignite a Culture of Innovation. https://elisabethbostwick.com/2020/11/10/ embracing-a-mindset-of-gratitude/

Brown, J., & Wong, J. (2017, June 6). How gratitude changes you and your brain. Greater Good; The Greater Good Science Center at the University of California, Berkeley. https://greatergood.berkeley.edu/article/item/ how_gratitude_changes_you_and_your_brain

Campbell, J. (n.d.). *Stop the negative self talk! Thank your body with this gratitude meditation.* YouAligned. https://youaligned.com/mindfulness/body-scan-gratitude-meditation/

Cartwright, D. (2021, February 12). *Gratitude affirmations to feel calm, happy and centered.* The Daily Shifts. https://www.thedailyshifts.com/blog/grati tude-affirmations-to-feel-calm-happy-and-centered

Cherry, K. (2021, October 29). *What is gratitude?* Verywell Mind. https://www. verywellmind.com/what-is-gratitude-5206817

Chowdhury, M. R. (2019, April 9). *The neuroscience of gratitude and effects on the brain.* Positive Psychology. https://positivepsychology.com/neuroscience-of-gratitude/

Clear, J. (n.d.). Habit stacking: *How to build new habits by taking advantage of old ones.* James Clear. https://jamesclear.com/habit-stacking

Conlon, C. (2023, March 24). *40 simple ways to practice gratitude.* Lifehack. https://www.lifehack.org/articles/communication/40-simple-ways-prac tice-gratitude.html

The Counseling Teacher. (n.d.). *5 ways to reframe negative thoughts.* Confident

Counselors. https://confidentcounselors.com/2018/03/19/reframe-nega tive-thoughts/

Dawn. (2019, September 22). *Why gratitude is the key to unlocking happiness and success.* Stepping Stones to Financial Independence. https://steppingston estofi.com/gratitude-happiness-success/

Emma-Louise. (2023, May 24). *Coaching tools 101: Boost confidence with this easy, fun "role model" coaching exercise!* The Coaching Tools Company. https://www.thecoachingtoolscompany.com/coaching-tools-101-boost-confidence-coaching-exercise-with-role-models-emma-louise-elsey

Emmons, R. (2013, May 13). *How gratitude can help you through hard times.* Greater Good. https://greatergood.berkeley.edu/article/item/how_gratitude_can_help_you_through_hard_times

Emmons, R. A., & McCullough, M. E. (2003). Counting blessings versus burdens: An experimental investigation of gratitude and subjective well-being in daily life. *Journal of Personality and Social Psychology, 84*(2), 377–389. https://doi.org/10.1037/0022-3514.84.2.377

EmpathyLab. (2022, March 5). *Gratitude and empathy.* EmpathyLab. https://www.empathylab.uk/gratitude-and-empathy

Fostering a positive self-image. (2020, November 24). Cleveland Clinic. https://my.clevelandclinic.org/health/articles/12942-fostering-a-positive-self-image

Gavin, MD, M. L. (2018, August). *Gratitude (for teens).* Kidshealth. https://kidshealth.org/en/teens/gratitude.html

Goldberg, M. (n.d.). *Exactly how to find joy today—and every day.* Oprah Daily. https://www.oprahdaily.com/life/health/a32957825/how-to-find-joy/

Gratitube. (2020, August 19). *Gratitude is a self esteem boost for us all.* Medium. https://medium.com/@Gratitube/gratitude-is-a-self-esteem-boost-for-us-all-3608995d07cb

Gratitude Quotes. (n.d.). Jesuit Resource. https://www.xavier.edu/jesuitre source/online-resources/quote-archive1/gratitude

Haden, J. (2014, September 12). *40 inspiring motivational quotes about gratitude.* Inc.Africa. https://incafrica.com/library/jeff-haden-40-inspiring-motiva tional-quotes-about-gratitude

The Healthy Minds Team. (2021, August 3). *Well-Being tip: Get a gratitude buddy.* Healthy Minds Innovations. https://hminnovations.org/blog/learn-practice/tuesday-tip-get-a-gratitude-buddy

Houston, E. (2019, April 9). *How to express gratitude to others: 19 examples &*

ideas. Positive Psychology. https://positivepsychology.com/how-to-express-gratitude/

How gratitude can help you sleep at night. (2022, November 15). Silent Night Therapy. https://www.sleepbetterny.com/how-gratitude-can-help-you-sleep-at-night/

How to add gratitude to your daily routine. (n.d.). Artis Senior Living. https://artisseniorliving.com/blog/how-to-add-gratitude-to-your-daily-routine/

HT Lifestyle Desk. (2023, January 9). *How to practice the art of finding joy in little things.* Hindustan Times. https://www.hindustantimes.com/lifestyle/health/how-to-practice-the-art-of-finding-joy-in-little-things-101673271776357.html

Huffman, J. C., Beale, E. E., Beach, S. R., Celano, C. M., Belcher, A. M., Moore, S. V., Suarez, L., Gandhi, P. U., Motiwala, S. R., Gaggin, H., & Januzzi, J. L. (2015). Design and baseline data from the gratitude research in acute coronary events (GRACE) study. *Contemporary Clinical Trials, 44,* 11–19. https://doi.org/10.1016/j.cct.2015.07.002

Huijer, H. (2023, January 29). *The powerful relationship between gratitude and happiness (with actual examples).* Tracking Happiness. https://www.trackinghappiness.com/how-does-gratitude-make-us-happier-with-actual-examples/

Hull, M. (Ed.). (2022, May 26). *Insomnia facts and statistics.* The Recovery Village. https://www.therecoveryvillage.com/mental-health/insomnia/insomnia-statistics/

Kemp, R. (2021, September 1). *Why gratitude gives rise to contentment, empathy, and humility.* LinkedIn. https://www.linkedin.com/pulse/why-gratitude-gives-rise-contentment-empathy-humility-ryan-kemp/

Kemper, Dr. K. (2023). *Gratitude meditation (greater good in action).* Berkeley. https://ggia.berkeley.edu/practice/gratitude_meditation

Khorrami, N. (2020a, June 24). *Why expressing gratitude strengthens our relationships.* Psychology Today. https://www.psychologytoday.com/us/blog/comfort-gratitude/202006/why-expressing-gratitude-strengthens-our-relationships

Khorrami, N. (2020b, July 7). *Gratitude helps minimize feelings of stress.* Psychology Today. https://www.psychologytoday.com/us/blog/comfort-gratitude/202007/gratitude-helps-minimize-feelings-stress

Lebow, H. (2021, July 12). *How mindfulness and gratitude go hand in hand.* Psych

Central. https://psychcentral.com/blog/how-gratitude-and-mindfulness-go-hand-in-hand

Lee, M., Lee, J., Park, B.-J., & Miyazaki, Y. (2015). Interaction with indoor plants may reduce psychological and physiological stress by suppressing autonomic nervous system activity in young adults: A randomized cross-over study. *Journal of Physiological Anthropology, 34*(1). https://doi.org/10.1186/s40101-015-0060-8

Mayo Clinic Staff. (2022, February 3). *Positive thinking: Stop negative self-talk to reduce stress.* Mayo Clinic. https://www.mayoclinic.org/healthy-lifestyle/stress-management/in-depth/positive-thinking/art-20043950

Millacci, T. S. (2023, February 22). *What is gratitude and why is it so important?* Positive Psychology. https://positivepsychology.com/gratitude-appreciation/

Miller, K. D. (2023, April 19). *14 benefits of practicing gratitude (incl. journaling).* Positive Psychology. https://positivepsychology.com/benefits-of-gratitude/#what-are-the-benefits-of-gratitude

Mills, P. J., Redwine, L., Wilson, K., Pung, M. A., Chinh, K., Greenberg, B. H., Lunde, O., Maisel, A., Raisinghani, A., Wood, A., & Chopra, D. (2015). The role of gratitude in spiritual well-being in asymptomatic heart failure patients. *Spirituality in Clinical Practice, 2*(1), 5–17. https://doi.org/10.1037/scp0000050

Mindful eating. (2020, September). Harvard T.H. Chan. https://www.hsph.harvard.edu/nutritionsource/mindful-eating/

Mishra, S. (2021, November 29). *Viral two passengers on bus cartoon triggers meme fest online. best ones.* India Today. https://www.indiatoday.in/trending-news/story/viral-two-passengers-on-bus-cartoon-triggers-meme-fest-online-best-ones-1882049-2021-11-29

Moss, H. (n.d.). *How to shift your mindset by being more grateful.* Wise Waves. https://wisewaves.uk/shift-mindset-be-more-grateful/

Moyo, J. (2021, January 29). *Gratitude practice for positive change and perspective.* My Inspiration Studio. https://myinspirationstudio.com/blogs/inspo-hub/gratitude-breathing-to-try-today

Neighmond, P. (2015, November 23). *Gratitude is good for the soul and helps the heart, too.* NPR. https://www.npr.org/sections/health-shots/2015/11/23/456656055/gratitude-is-good-for-the-soul-and-it-helps-the-heart-too

Onitsuka, T., Shenton, M. E., Salisbury, D. F., Dickey, C. C., Kasai, K., Toner, S. K., Frumin, M., Kikinis, R., Jolesz, F. A., & McCarley, R. W. (2004).

Middle and inferior temporal gyrus gray matter volume abnormalities in chronic schizophrenia: An MRI study. *American Journal of Psychiatry, 161*(9), 1603–1611. https://doi.org/10.1176/appi.ajp.161.9.1603

Page, S. (2022, January 13). *57 quotes on wellness and health to inspire healthy living.* Total Wellness. https://info.totalwellnesshealth.com/blog/quotes-on-wellness-and-health

The Partnership In Education. (2021). *Heartbeat: A mindfulness exercise to calm your emotions* [Video]. YouTube. https://youtu.be/3iUf73v92lI

Pedersen, E., & Lieberman, D. (2017, December 6). *How gratitude helps your friendships grow.* Greater Good. https://greatergood.berkeley.edu/article/item/how_gratitude_helps_your_friendships_grow

Perry, E. (2022, February 23). *You've earned it: Learn about the benefits of rewarding yourself.* BetterUp. https://www.betterup.com/blog/reward-yourself

Raman, N. (2019, July 16). *5 reasons why consistency is an important habit.* Neel Raman Inspiring Greatness. https://neelraman.com/5-reasons-why-consistency-is-an-important-habit/

Raypole, C. (2021, February 5). *Breaking down the habit loop.* Healthline. https://www.healthline.com/health/mental-health/habit-loop

Reframing unhelpful thoughts. (n.d.). NHS. https://www.nhs.uk/every-mind-matters/mental-wellbeing-tips/self-help-cbt-techniques/reframing-unhelpful-thoughts/

Regan, S. (2021, December 11). *Struggle with self-love? Why you might want to look at yourself in the mirror.* Mindbodygreen. https://www.mindbodygreen.com/articles/mirror-work

Rush University Medical Center. (2018, February 14). *Everyday activities associated with more gray matter in brains of older adults: Study measured amount of lifestyle physical activity such as house work, dog walking and gardening.* ScienceDaily. https://www.sciencedaily.com/releases/2018/02/180214093828.htm

Sabrina. (n.d.). *How to be grateful in hard times: Embrace these 5 habits.* The Budding Optimist. https://buddingoptimist.com/how-to-be-grateful-in-hard-times/

Scott, E. (2020, September 30). *The benefits of cultivating gratitude for stress relief.* Verywell Mind. https://www.verywellmind.com/the-benefits-of-gratitude-for-stress-relief-3144867

Shah, S. (2020, November 23). *Gratitude yoga - 8 yoga poses that kindle gratitude on thanksgiving.* Art of Living. https://www.artofliving.org/us-en/grati tude-yoga-8-yoga-poses-that-kindle-gratitude-on-thanksgiving

Sharpe, R. (2021, February 2). *50 gratitude quotes to help you feel thankful.* Declutter the Mind. https://declutterthemind.com/blog/gratitude-quotes/

Shutterfly Community. (2020, June 26). *50 inspiring gratitude quotes.* Shutterfly. https://www.shutterfly.com/ideas/gratitude-quotes

Simon-Thomas, E. (2012, December 19). *A "thnx" a day keeps the doctor away.* Greater Good. https://greatergood.berkeley.edu/article/item/ a_thnx_a_day_keeps_the_doctor_away

Smith, A. J. (2021, August 11). *Gratitude - A mental health game changer.* Anxiety and Depression Association of America. https://adaa.org/learn-from-us/ from-the-experts/blog-posts/consumer/gratitude-mental-health-game-changer

Smith, E.-M. (2022, March 25). *Create a positivity jar to remember good times.* HealthyPlace. https://www.healthyplace.com/self-help/positivity/create-a-positivity-jar-to-remember-good-times

Spector, N. (2018, September 26). *This daily gratitude routine can train your brain to be happier.* NBC News. https://www.nbcnews.com/better/health/ daily-gratitude-routine-can-train-your-brain-be-happier-ncna912961

Staff Wellbeing. (2017, November 9). *Integrating gratitude into daily life.* Move This World. https://www.movethisworld.com/staff-wellbeing/integrat ing-gratitude-into-daily-life/

Suttie, J. (2021, August 9). *Does practicing gratitude help your immune system?* Greater Good. https://greatergood.berkeley.edu/article/item/ does_practicing_gratitude_help_your_immune_system

Sutton, J. (2019, April 9). *What is mindfulness? Definition, benefits and psychology.* Positive Psychology. https://positivepsychology.com/what-is-mindfulness/

Team Soulveda. (2023, May 6). *I am grateful: The power of gratitude in over-coming adversity.* Soulveda. https://www.soulveda.com/happiness/the-power-of-gratitude-in-overcoming-adversity/

Teh, D. (2019, September 4). *4 ways to practice gratitude and build resilience.* Thrive Global. https://community.thriveglobal.com/4-ways-to-practice-gratitude-and-build-resilience/

10 amazing statistics to celebrate national gratitude month. (2020, October 20).

Halo. https://halo.com/10-amazing-statistics-to-celebrate-national-gratitude-month/

10 top ways to practice gratitude during difficult times. (n.d.). Thnks. https://www.thnks.com/blog/practice-gratitude-during-difficult-times

Tewari, A. (n.d.). *How to make a vision board that really works.* Gratitude Blog. https://blog.gratefulness.me/all-you-need-to-create-your-vision-board-today/

30 gratitude quotes for health, happiness and healing. (n.d.). Virtues for Life. https://www.virtuesforlife.com/30-gratitude-quotes-health-happiness-healing/

Thompson, J. (2020, March 29). *Resilience and the practice of gratitude.* Psychology Today. https://www.psychologytoday.com/intl/blog/beyond-words/202003/resilience-and-the-practice-gratitude

Tomczyk, J., Nezlek, J. B., & Krejtz, I. (2022). Gratitude can help women at-risk for depression accept their depressive symptoms, which leads to improved mental health. *Frontiers in Psychology, 13.* https://doi.org/10.3389/fpsyg.2022.878819

Top 10 tips for a good night's rest. (n.d.). British Heart Foundation. https://www.bhf.org.uk/informationsupport/heart-matters-magazine/wellbeing/sleeping-tips

Villines, Z. (2019, February 25). *10 serotonin deficiency symptoms everyone should look out for.* Good Therapy. https://www.goodtherapy.org/blog/10-serotonin-deficiency-symptoms-everyone-should-look-out-for-0225197

Wong, Y. J., Owen, J., Gabana, N. T., Brown, J. W., McInnis, S., Toth, P., & Gilman, L. (2016). Does gratitude writing improve the mental health of psychotherapy clients? Evidence from a randomized controlled trial. *Psychotherapy Research, 28*(2), 192–202. https://doi.org/10.1080/10503307.2016.1169332

Writing a letter to your future self: Benefits, guide, and template. (2023, February 17). Reflection.app. https://www.reflection.app/blog/writing-a-letter-to-my-future-self

Yuen, C. (2021, January 27). *Why mood tracking could be your answer for avoiding burnout.* Greatist. https://greatist.com/grow/mood-tracking-journal

Printed in Great Britain
by Amazon